Sam's Story

Vijitha Yapa Publications
Unity Plaza, 2 Galle Road, Colombo 4, Sri Lanka
Tel. (94 1) 596960   Fax (94 1) 584801
e-mail: vijiyapa@sri.lanka.net

Copyright © Elmo Jayawardena

ISBN 955 8095 09 5

All rights reserved. No part of this book may be reproduced or utilized in any form or by any means, electronic or mechancal including photocopying, recording or by any information storage retrieval system, without permission in writing from the publishers.

First Edition September 2001
First Reprint July 2002
Second Reprint March 2003

Cover by
Dineli, Mevan & Sujith

Printed by
Piyasiri Printing Systems, Nugegoda

Sam's Story

by

Elmo Jayawardena

Vijitha Yapa Publications
Sri Lanka

To Dil, Dineli and Mevan

PREFACE

How would you like to be remembered? By your wealth, by your acquisitions or by the fact that your life touched someone else's? And made it that much better for it. The arts and sciences have always been avenues where the milestones mark every interaction between the giver and the recipient.

For writers, like Elmo Jayawardena, their words are their best bet for posterity. It is with this awesome responsibility that Elmo took up his task of narrating Sam's story. A story about a simple village bumpkin who learns to come to terms with city life and life itself. You cannot but be moved by the trials and tribulations even as you laugh at Sam's bumbling ways.

In today's world there is no such thing as true fiction. For the story teller, life's experiences are his grist and the combination of the truth and the imagination is where he most delicately reflects the power and the glory of his pen.

Sam's Story fulfils these requirements and brings to the fore the intimacy of the locale as well as the true-to-life characters in the book. It is written with a keen insight, a constant flair for the language and a sense of restraint that gives the book its depth and its cadence.

It comes as no surprise to me that the book has been awarded the Graetiaen Prize for the most outstanding work in English by a Sri Lankan. I am confident that its success will spur a new slew of Anglo-Lankan writers to create a durable and abiding dimension to this genre of writing. It is praiseworthy that Sam's Story will be translated into Sinhala and Tamil for good literature knows no boundaries and must be encouraged to appeal to the widest audience.

With two other books in the pipeline, Elmo Jayawardena is poised for great things and I look forward to adding both "The Last Kingdom of Sinhalay" and "This is your Captain Speaking" to my collection when they are released.

Patrick Michael
Editor
Weekend magazine
Khaleej Times

Dubai - UAE

"There are different meanings to life"

Contents

River house	9
Piya	25
The Boy	35
Kaluwa	44
Leandro	50
Elections	66
Christmas	74
My war	96
The Girl	119
Everyone	139
Colombo	156
Back to the beginning	162

Sam's Story

River House

I came to work at the river house not so long ago. It was a few years before the world became 2000. Two thousand to me is a nice sounding number, that is why I remember, like twenty-five. I know the exact month too when all this started. It was the mango month. That is how everybody in our village called it - mango month.

We always had our own names for the months. That way it was easy to remember how the years came and went. Mango month, raining month, dry month, mangosteen month, first month, last month and so on it went. Mango month was when there were more green mangoes than green leaves in the branches of the mango trees.

That's when I first came to the river house.

'Can you cook?' the Master in the river house asked me.

'Can you iron clothes?'

'Can you do the marketing; buy vegetables, buy bread, buy beef?'

One after the other the questions came, like thunderclaps.

I never could figure out why people asked me so many questions. Maybe they thought I knew all the answers to life. Even when I stood at a bus stop, someone would ask me some stupid question.

'What time will the next bus come?'

People always asked me things like that. How would I know when the next bus is coming?

'When did the last bus go?'

That is a real stupid question. I wouldn't be here if I had been at the bus stop when the last bus went - would I?

Some even ask me, 'Are you waiting for a bus?'

'No, I'm waiting for a boat,' I would softly mutter under my breath.

I think people like to ask questions. I don't mind that. But why pick on me? I don't like questions. As long as I remember, it had been that way with me. My life has always been simple. No questions, no answers. Just take it as it comes.

I never looked for answers in life. What's the point? They would seldom be the ones I want them to be. No, I never worried about knowing what the answers were. Maybe that is why I didn't like questions.

'How old?'

'What do you do?'

'You have brothers? Sisters?' People would ask me many more like that. Those were rather the common and easy ones.

There were more difficult ones too.

'Are you a fool? Are you dumb?'

Yes, they asked me things like that. What can I say? Even if I am a fool do you think I will say yes? How many dumb people do you know who would say they are dumb? See what I mean about these questions? Just asked for the sake of asking. That's why I don't like them. That is why I do not like when people ask so many questions from me.

The funny thing is when some idiot asked me something I would take some time to answer. Then he would keep looking at me as if his very life depended on what I said.

Sam's Story

There were some answers I knew for sure. I had two sisters and two brothers and an old mother who tapped rubber to put food on our table. That's the only reply I gave to anybody who asked me questions. That part I was sure of. The rest of it was always so vague.

'How old?'

How would I know when I was born? I was too young to note and remember. And then again, nobody told me about how and when I came to this world. Even if they did, I would forget.

'What can you do?'

What a stupid question. I can do so many things. How to list? I have lived this long in my life doing many things. Of course these people who ask me questions always look at me in a strange manner. If I do not answer they get annoyed. If I answer and if my reply is different to the one they expected, they look disappointed. They stare at me in a funny way. Somehow this makes me feel that I am confusing them. I am used to it, like so many other things in my life. Sometimes I think I am different. Often I feel so. Maybe that is why they give me strange looks.

Even when I first went to the village school, I remember the same look.

At the beginning, the old teacher and some of the children who came from other villages looked at me that way. I have seen it so often I even have an idea what it is all about. I think this look belongs to people when they see me for the first time. It takes awhile for them to get used to me. No, no, I am not ugly, definitely not as ugly as Leandro. Its got nothing to do with the way my face is. Maybe it is the way I speak. Sometimes some words spit out of my lips with a hissing noise, like the air pump in the bicycle shop. 'Shu shu shu,' some noise like that.

Back in my village, they never do that; I mean the funny look business. Must be because the people in our village were used to me. I grew up there. They were always there and I was always there.

Our villagers were not strangers, not first-timers like the schoolteacher and the children from other villages, or like my new Master in the river house. Well, that is not my story. I am as usual jumping rails. What I mean is that I started telling you about this new river house and my new job as a houseboy and went in a circle about the strange ways people look at me. How stupid!

My new Master in the river house was no different. The first time we met, out came the questions. First he asked me whether I could cook and all those kind of questions I mentioned at the beginning. Then he came out with some special ones.

'Have you worked before?' The Master asked me.

I told him 'Yes' and told him all about Madam Martell and her house in Colombo. She was a white lady from a far away land who had a thin tall white husband who played cards all the time.

'How old are you?'

I told him twenty-five, the number always sounded nice to me. I like twenty-five, same as two thousand. I like two thousand also.

Then the Master wanted to know how long I worked for Madam Martell. I told him twenty-five again. He gave me a strange look and laughed.

'Did you go to work straight from the hospital?' The Master asked me and then he laughed loud.

I didn't know why, but I laughed too. Anyway, I got the job. He said I was in charge of everything in the house.

'Sam, I am the Big Boss here,' he gestured wide with his hands

Sam's Story

like a platform politician and laughed again. I also kept laughing.
'You can call me Boss.'
'You are the Small Boss,' he gestured again, still laughing and this time going in a smaller circle with his hands. We both continued like that - laughing together.

We must have appeared like two mad men, he in his own joke and I in my 'no' joke. Big Boss and Small Boss, each laughing away for his own reasons, with the other not knowing why or what it was all about.

Life was easy in the river house. I was the 'Small Boss' as the Master said. I did everything. I swept the garden; I watered the flowerbeds and the lawn. I washed the cars. I opened the gate when the cars came and closed the gate when the cars went. I fed the dogs and switched the house and garden lights on in the evening and switched them off in the morning.

The lights were simple to remember. Down is "on", up is "off".

I loved that business of switching lights. There were so many lights in the river house. I don't know why, but most of them we never used. They were fixed everywhere and they came in all kinds. Bright ones and light ones and even small ones that gave more darkness than light. They all had different switches.

Down is "on", up is "off". Easy, how to forget that?

There were so many lights in the garden too, in different colours, hidden in the flower bushes. They made the garden trees glow in blue, red, yellow and green. The lights were very badly hidden. Though you couldn't see the bulbs, you didn't have much problems knowing where they were. The glow in the garden bushes gave away where the light bulbs were hiding.

I think it was a bit stupid.

Other than switching lights, my favourite job in the river house was watering the garden. I loved the long yellow hose and the sprouting water. I would open the tap, drag the hose near the plants, aim and fire. I could make various patterns with my big finger and send the water flow any way I chose; hard, soft, wide, narrow, anything. I loved that.

I would send the water hard on the anthuriums. I didn't like them. They looked vulgar, with that thing sticking out as if it had been having dirty thoughts. But I was always gentle with the shoe flowers. I liked their colours, bright and cheerful, like my mood when I watered the garden.

Every afternoon I would watch the sky like a hawk, looking for clouds and rain. I didn't want to miss my watering. I didn't mind the rain, I could go out and yet water the plants in the rain. But the Madam said it was useless.

'Don't water the plants when it rains, Sammy.'

She never told me why.

My Master's house was big. Everything there was big; the garden was big, the river was big. Even the room where Leandro cooked was big. Leandro was not my friend. He was the cook in the river house. Leandro was short and ugly and was a bit stupid. He belonged to the other kind. So was Janet, the housemaid. But Janet was not like Leandro; she was a little better. She hardly spoke, just did her work and combed her hair whenever she had nothing to do. She had very long hair, always oiled and always combed. Janet wasn't bad looking either; she had those things, a bit jutting out from the front of her blouse, but always well covered.

Leandro and Janet were both from the kind that made war and killed soldiers and threw bombs at our leaders. I didn't like them. If I knew I had to work with their kind, I would not have come to the river house. But I was here; I couldn't go back, nothing to go back to in the village. That's another story, I'll tell you later about that part as I go along.

Bhurus was my best friend. He was the dog in the river house. He was a boxing dog; brown and black lines on his skin. Bhurus had no tail. I think some stupid man had cut it when he was a baby dog. He now had a little stump that he wagged with vigour whenever he saw me. He was very ugly, with a big ugly mouth and no nose. But I loved Bhurus. He loved me too. We spent a lot of time together. Every time I called him 'Bhurus, Bhurus, Bhurus' the Master's daughter would come shouting.

'No no Sam, it is not Bhurus, it is BRUTUS.'

She would make her eyes big and give this funny growling sound; she called it rolling. She would start by tightening her mouth and extending her lips into a small round hole saying 'brrrr-ouuuuu' and then go 'TUS' like breaking a stick. 'Brutus, Brutus, Brutus,' she would repeat the sound for my benefit.

I never could get that funny sounding name. After awhile she gave up. She stopped trying to correct me whenever I called my friend. I am not sure but I think she knew I was right. Once or twice I heard her ignoring her round mouth "ooos" and stick breaking "tusses" and calling my friend the way I did - Bhurus.

Bhurus of course didn't mind. I don't think he cared very much about this business of how he was called.

When I said 'Bhurus, come, come,' he came. I think he liked my name better, Bhurus.

The other dog was Lena. She was beautiful; she was tall and had a brown shining coat. Lena didn't run around like the stupid Bhurus. She minded her business and slept most of the time. In her own way she was nice. Bhurus and Lena were my friends. They didn't throw bombs. They didn't kill any people.

16

I liked my Boss's house by the river. It had a large garden. The outside was painted white and the inside had different colours for different rooms. The floor was red, polished red, lines this way and lines that way, all in perfect squares. That was downstairs. Upstairs had wood on the floor in some places and tiles in other places. I do not know why that is. They must have run out of tiles and finished the job with wood, or they may have even run out of wood and finished the job with tiles. Something must have run out but they managed nicely. Not just mixed, but room by room, some wood, some tile.

There were bathrooms everywhere in the river house. Each bedroom had one. We had ours next to the garage, for Leandro, Janet and me. I was the one who cleaned them all. That's how I became a good bathroom man.

The inside of the river house was big, so many different sections, different rooms for different things. To eat, there was one place, to talk, another place, to watch television an entire room, to read books another place. At the beginning I always got confused with all these separate sections of the house. Back where I came from, in our village, most houses had only one room. We did everything there, within four walls. I mean not real walls but more like half-rotted planks, but no confusion. The Boss' river house was a different place; too many rooms.

The area where the river house people ate and sat to talk and drink, the walls were painted nicely in a cream colour. But for some reason they were all mostly covered with something or the other. There were many pictures hanging on them. Each one pasted in a wide wooden frame. Some were glass covered, some just plain. There were paint pictures of all kinds; of flowers and trees, of hills with blue skies and seas with black skies, of ships sailing and birds flying; all kinds of pictures. There were women too, white women in big pictures; beautiful, shy women with their dresses falling from their chests or lifting above their knees and showing those shy parts of their bodies. They only showed little, maybe half, not the real thing, not worth hanging on a wall and looking.

Where there were no pictures, there were so many other things covering the wall. No wall was empty. There were small carpets in bright colours, larger carpets with dull colours hanging by long nails. There were shining brass curved knives and long brass swords, all fixed to polished wooden planks and stuck on the wall. In some places there were ugly looking masks and in other places there were many pictures of their God.

One wall was filled only with pictures of the family. Those pictures were all when the children were babies and the Master and the Madam were young. I think they have taken the good ones and put them there to make the Master and Madam look good. Young and pretty, black hair and thin and always smiling.

That's how the walls were in the river house.

Even the pillars inside the house had various things hanging on them.

Now you get an idea what my new house was like? Let me tell you some more.

The riverside of my Master's house was all glass; large glass windows on wooden frames that rolled to the sides on noisy little wheels. We could move the windows out of the way and open the house to get the river breeze. When the windows were rolled out, the river could be clearly seen by anyone sitting in the living room.

'That's how we wanted it Sam, to look at the river,' my Boss told me that.

I don't know why they wanted to keep looking at the river. It was the same river; it flowed slow and looked the same everyday.

The house had chairs everywhere. There were chairs to sit and drink, chairs to read newspapers, chairs to watch cricket matches on television, chairs to relax and look at the river. It was like the rooms; almost everything had its own special chair.

There were many bedrooms too; each one in the house had their own sleeping place. All except Master and Madam and Leandro and I. We are the ones who shared rooms. Master and Madam had a big room that could be cooled. Leandro and I had a smaller room, but no cooling. Master's daughter, the Girl, had a room and so did the Master's son, the one I call the Boy. Our Janet too had her own. Her room was the tiniest in the house, just big enough to keep her small bed and her old green canvas bag where she kept everything in the world that belonged to her.

My room was nice; I mean our room - Leandro's and mine. It had a large window and I could see the river and see the fishing boats as they went past our house. All that was good. The only problem was Leandro. I hated sharing the room with him.

Most things he did annoyed me. I hated when Leandro washed and hung his multicoloured *lankets*. His normal washing he hung outside, but his *lankets* he always hung inside the room as if he didn't want anyone to know what he wore under his sarong to protect his things. Leandro had a string drawn right across the room to hang his *lankets*. They hung on it to dry. Red, green and all colours, they hung there like dead bats. Big holes for the legs, a big hole for his fat waist and a little piece of cloth to hold his things. Those were his *lankets,* constantly dripping water and wetting our room floor; hanging like dead bats on current wires.

Sam's Story

I had to be very careful when I walked, I didn't want that cloth to touch my face, specially the part that held his things.

There was another problem that bothered me in sharing the room with this fool. Leandro farted. I have never seen someone who farted so much and so loud. Leandro's farts varied and had their own tunes. Some slow dragged "ppppeeeee" like a note from an old snake charmer's horn, and others went "boom" like gunshots. It was annoying.

I hated his farts, I hated his wet *lankets*, and I hated him. Anyway I had no choice; Leandro remained my roommate, though many a time I secretly wished it was Janet.

The garden of the river house went all the way to the river, all grass and many trees. Many trees meant many leaves fell. I had to sweep many times to keep the garden clean. In no time I became a champion garden sweeping man.

At the beginning itself our Madam very seriously told me everything about sweeping the garden and what to do with the dirt. 'Sammy boy, don't put dirt into the river, collect them into the garbage bags.' She always called me Sammy boy.

I don't know why she was worried about collecting dirt into bags and not throwing it all into the river. We always did that in our village. She spoke as if the river would mind. Every time she saw me sweeping the garden she kept repeating the same thing.

'Sammy boy, don't put dirt into the river.'

One day no one was at home. I swept the entire garden and collected a lot of dirt, mostly fallen leaves. I threw all that into the river, just to see what would happen. Nothing happened. The dirt got swallowed by the water and drifted down. I carefully watched till it all disappeared. I wanted to tell the Madam that nothing happens when you put dirt into the river. But Janet stopped me.

'Don't be stupid Sam, don't tell them everything that happens here.' That's what she said. I didn't want to be stupid.

She said it is better we take dirt in the garbage bag to the place where they dumped all the rot. That was fine, it suited me. It was I who mostly went in the van to throw the garbage bags. I always enjoyed those van rides. I got selected to do them fairly and squarely. That is what Leandro said; democratically, he used these big words. I always won the vote to carry the garbage.

Come to think of it, voting was big among the three of us. Leandro Janet and me, we voted on everything. Leandro said that is how things are done when you need to do things properly. You vote. He said our leaders always got voted to run the country. That was big stuff. Ours was small, kitchen vote, but to us it was very important. Most times I lost, so what? I didn't mind. Sometimes I also won.

Every evening we voted in what language we would watch the television - Sinhala or Tamil. It was our television, fixed in the kitchen. Leandro would take a box of matches and pick three matchsticks. He would break them in two and give each of us both parts. Stick only and stick and black. He would then take a cup and tell us to throw in the cup our vote. Stick only is Sinhala, stick and black is Tamil. We threw our choice and he shook the cup up and down like a magic man and poured the result out. I do not know how, but it was always a Tamil win.

But sometimes I too won the voting. I noticed that it happened mostly when Janet was not in the competition; it was about things like who takes the garbage and who cleans the toilet. The competition was strictly Leandro against me. But all three voted. It is democratic. I am sure at such times Janet voted for me and I got elected. I beat Leandro every time. Many times I did get the feeling she had a soft corner for me. She was nice. But the

Sam's Story

problem was we were different. Janet was from the side that threw bombs.

They both told me that we must not tell the Madam about our voting.

'We must sort things out democratically, like our leaders,' they explained very seriously.

That was fine. I kept my mouth shut. Democratic voting was fine with me. I won some and lost some. In the ones I won, like cleaning the toilets, sometimes I got all three votes. Even Leandro voted for me. The ones I lost I didn't mind, specially the television. People on television always spoke so fast. I could never understand what they were saying or what was going on; never mind in what language it was said.

Harrison too was a big player in the river house. He drove the vehicles in the river house. It was through him that I came to work for my Master. Harrison's older brother drove a "tuk-tuk" three-wheeler in the city and this brother's woman was from our village. My sister Loku and this woman went to school together. That's how Harrison came to know of me and arranged the job, all by connections.

Apart from driving, Harrison took care of everything that needed to be done that was beyond Janet, Leandro and me. It was always Harrison, for things the river house needed from outside its walls. Inside, it was the three of us.

'Harrison go there, Harrison buy fish, Harrison go and pay the telephone bill, Harrison bring the carpenter, Harrison bring the plumber,' that's how the outside orders went.

He was good at getting things done. My Master always called him "Friday Man" even though he did things everyday of the week.

Harrison came in the morning and went in the evening. He had a house and a family who lived not so far away. He was the one who drove the van when I went to drop the garbage.

Sometimes Harrison stayed the night when Master and Madam were away and only Janet, Leandro and I were in the river house. He got extra pay for that. That's what he told me. Nice job; got paid to sleep. He was the boss when Master and Madam were out. I mean he was the real boss. I was the boss for the work. Leandro was nothing. Only a stupid cook. Janet of course is a woman, so she never counted.

I almost forgot. It is the Master's son, the Boy. After Bhurus and Lena, he was the best. He was a tall pretty boy, always smiling. From the very first day we met he liked me and I liked him. He was the one who spoke with me most in the river house.

'Sammy, what's the scene?'

That's what he always said.

'Sammy, how's it going man?' - that was his next line.

We did a lot of things together. We went in the boat, we went in his car, we sometimes caught fish together, many things. There was always something happening when the Boy was around.

Often we used to wear hats and go in the rowing boat. It was a long red boat with two seats. The Boy had named it "*Solitaire*" and that name was written in big yellow letters in front of the boat. The Boy rowed the red boat and I sat and watched. That's the way he wanted it.

'You relax Sam, I'll row, it's good for my muscles,' he grinned and repeated the words often.

I always enjoyed going in the boat with him. We spoke about a lot of things. He rowed and spoke and I mostly listened. It was quiet in the river, nobody disturbed. There was no noise, only the waves slapping on the side of our "*Solitaire*".

Sam's Story

He used to ask me about my life in the village. What I did before I came to his father's house. I told him many things, about my home, about my mother tapping rubber, about my brothers Jaya and Madiya and my two sisters Loku and Podi. I also told him about my friend Piya and how he drowned the day the river overflowed. I told him whatever I could remember. I kept some back too. My mother had told me not to talk about them.

The Boy always said that when he grew old he would take me to work for him. 'Don't worry Sammy, I'll take care of you.'

I knew he meant it.

My life was always full when the Boy was at home. He had many friends and they came often to the river house. We had a lot of fun. His friends were also like him. They laughed easily and they didn't give me strange looks. I think the Boy had told them that I was his friend. That made it easy. That is how his friends became my friends.

My Boss' two children came to the river house only for their holidays. The Boy and his sister were learning in a far away land. Like Madam Martell's land; very far. You have to fly there in a thing called the aerobblane; too far to walk, too far even to go by car. Harrison told me that. He mentioned some name for the place, but I have forgotten.

That was how life was for me in the river house. I had three good friends, Bhurus, Lena and the Boy. I had more than enough to eat and a nice room to sleep. No problems, just days that passed nice and simple. My time was spent in switching lights, sweeping the garden, watering the plants, opening and closing the gate, things like that.

I had only one enemy, Leandro and one half enemy. No, that is not right. Janet was not half, maybe a quarter enemy, that too only because she was from the other kind.

Even both of them put together would only be a very small problem.

My life never had real problems. I could never figure out what a problem was. That's why I never had problems.

Piya

My village where I grew up was also by a river. It was a big river, just like the one near my Master's house. But my house was not as big as my Master's house. My house was small, just one room, very small. I think it was smaller than Leandro's kitchen. It was all right. We used it only to sleep, and that too, mainly when it rained.

My mother was the 'Boss' in our house. I like that word. It was the first thing I learnt from my Master, this 'Boss' word. My mother did everything. Not that there was anything much to do. She cooked, when there were things to cook and pretended she was sick when she had nothing to cook. She scolded us and she beat us whenever she felt like it. That was the sum total. She cried too. Not often, but I have seen it happening quite often.

I never liked to see her cry. Many times I asked her why. She always shook her head like a gecko. Never told me why.

Maybe she thought I would cry too. But I don't cry easily. I don't know why people cry.

There were six of us. My mother always said too many mouths to feed and cursed my father. I think my father is dead. Maybe he had gone away from our village. I cannot remember him. I don't think I ever saw him. He had gone a long time ago. Maybe long before we were born. I don't know. But I never met him.

I am the eldest; then my sister, Loku, then my brother Jaya, then my younger sister, Podi and my little brother Madiya. I think they all had real names, but that's what we called them. In a way my mother was clever, I mean about bringing babies. She knew when to produce boys and when to produce girls. Boy, girl, boy, girl and ended with a boy. She must have been clever. But she didn't know when to stop. Too many mouths to feed, as she herself always said.

Our village had only a few houses. They were all located far from each other. Everybody knew that we were given the land long ago because we helped somebody become a leader in the government.

'He gave this free, for us to build our homes,' that is what everyone said.

It was not his land, but because he became a leader he could give us the government land free. All the houses in the village were gifts from this kind man. I don't know why, but people still cursed him, including my mother. They all said he had a lot of money now.

'Took care of himself and his friends. They are all very rich now,' my mother mumbled every time that man's name was mentioned.

'So what's wrong?' That is what I thought. He had become rich by going to the government. That is why he gave gifts to the people of the village. I didn't know why people still said bad things about him.

Most of the houses in our village were near the river. Come to think of it, that is where I learnt to throw dirt into the river. That's what we all did in the village. We threw everything into the river. It was easy. Nothing rotted; everything was thrown and went drifting down to whereever our river flowed. We even pissed

Sam's Story

and shat in it, squatting on the riverbank. Even the women did it, but they always squatted behind some bush, as if they had something to hide.

We had to walk a long distance from our village to reach the main road. Not to me, but it was difficult for most. They always grumbled. Said it took too long to reach the road. From there we could take a bus and go anywhere in the world. Of course we had to wait a long time for a bus to come. We were lucky if they stopped. You see, the buses were always full and the bus-man always cursed. Not the driver, but the other one who took our money and shouted at us to go inside. How to go, the bus was like a sardine tin?

My Master taught me that too. I mean this sardine tin business. I remember him once telling me. 'Sam, when anything is tight, it is like a tin of sardines.' I don't know what people have got to do with a sardine tin but I liked the sound of the word.

Now, when anything is tight, I say it is like a sardine tin.

That was about our road and the bus. We just got in and went to town. We got off and did our thing. We got into another bus and came. We walked home. So what is there to grumble?

The men in our village had only two jobs. They were not 'Small Boss' like me. They either tapped rubber or dug sand from the riverbed. That's all they could do. No other jobs were there for anybody in our village. The women also tapped rubber. That is what my mother did to feed our family. I once tried tapping rubber too. It was my mother who took me to meet the *Kangani*. He is the rubber tapping 'Boss'.

The *Kangani* took one look at me and shook his head. Then he grinned and spoke to my mother in a funny tone.

'Job for him? Why tap rubber? I think he should go to the big house and take the Planter Boss' job.'

Then his grin vanished as he shouted, 'Are you mad?'
For some reason he was not happy with me.

My mother pleaded with him to try me out at least for one day. The *Kangani* thought for a while, maybe finding it difficult to decide which job to give me, to tap rubber or the job of the Planter Boss. Later he said "OK".

'Don't forget, you have to do things I like also.' I heard him whisper.

I think he liked my mother. That is how I got my first job.

The *Kangani* gave me a knife and told me to cut the lines on the tree trunk. That is how they collected rubber. You cut the tree with a pointed knife and the milk flows. You fix a coconut shell for the milk to drip. It was easy.

I went running to my first tree and started work.

I cut the lines and saw the white rubber milk drip down. I cut many trees that morning, always running from one tree to the other. I ran the whole day, enjoying myself and cutting so many trees and getting lot of rubber.

But the man was not happy, I mean the *Kangani*. I don't know why. I thought I made everyone happy. I saw all the others who were tapping rubber giggle like little girls when they saw me running from tree to tree and cutting the lines.

The *Kangani* shouted at me for everyone to hear.

'What did you do you idiot? What do you think the coconut shells are for - to poke up your arse?"

I forgot to fix the coconut shells.

He kept shouting, calling me names. '*Buruwa, Gon Haraka!*' he said that and many other things to scold me.

'Get out of my sight you bloody fool!' That's how he finished me off in my first job.

Sam's Story

I hate being called names. I don't like being called a fool. So I went home. No more tapping rubber.

That night I heard my mother cry for a long time and curse my father again.

The only other job available in our village was to dig sand from the river.

That was not for me. I am scared of the water. I don't like the river except to piss and shit and to throw dirt. This sand business is hard work. You work from morning till the sun goes down. You stand in the river, up to your waist. You have a strong pole dug into the river floor, very firm. You hang your big basket on it. You have another basket, a small one. You bend and dig, take the sand into the small basket and fill your big basket. You have to do that about five times to fill the big basket. When it is filled, you take the big basket and hang the small basket on the pole. Then you carry the big basket and walk to the shore and climb the steep bank and empty the sand from the basket into a heap. You come back and you go back. You go back and you come back, whichever way you like to call it. From morning till the sun goes down. You bend under water and feel the cool and you rise up with the basket and feel the heat. Cool, warm, cool, warm, the whole day long.

The men who do this drink a lot. They have to. They drink *kasippu* in the morning before they start, just to keep the body warm in the morning chill of the water. They drink *kasippu* when they finish work because they are very tired.

It was mostly a matter of working from sunrise to sunset and drinking *kasippu*. The sand diggers usually went back to their homes half drunk.

Their day was over, finished by the setting sun.

Their troubles too were over, drowned by the *kasippu* they drank.

All the houses in our village were the same, rotting wood planks covered by a cadjan roof and the floor hardened by a mixture of mud and cow-dung. The only problem was when it rained. The mud and the dung would get wet and start dissolving. Smells horrible, even to me. We hated the rain for this and for many other reasons. We couldn't sleep out when it rained. Six of us were too much for the house. But we managed. I always managed.

We liked it when the skies were clear. The breeze from the river was always there and made everything cool. Our house was in the shade. Large rubber trees were everywhere. My favourite was the large mango tree that stood right in front of our home. It was my tree. It had many branches and many leaves and when the mangoes came in the Mango month there were more mangoes than leaves. I always loved to sit on the branches of my mango tree. I could sit there for hours. It was my world. When I became hungry, I ate mango. When I was thirsty, I ran to the river to drink. I often slept under the mango tree. Remember I said at the beginning that these were days when the sky was clear. Nice days. No rain.

It even made my mother happy. She smiled sometimes when the days were sunny.

The nearest house to our house was not far away. That was where my friend Piya lived. His name was not Piya, he told me. He said it was Piyadasa. They called him Piya because people thought Piyadasa was too long. I don't know how a name can be long; it is not like my garden hose in the river house. Now that is what you call long.

Why cut his name to Piya, just to make it short?

Sam's Story

Madam Martell did the same with my name. You see, my name is not really Sam. It is what that white woman I worked for called me; same problem, name too long. This is another thing I never could figure out; this long name business. I can understand if a name is ugly, like Leandro, but why talk about length and breadth in a name, like a paddy field.

I could see Piya's house from our door; part of it only. You see, there was this little shack between us. I mean, between his house and mine. That was their toilet. It was only for the women; like in that 'moving hall' I once went to. Piya and his father always went to the river to shit and piss. Piya's father built the toilet for his woman and their daughter. He was a nice man. He did not go away like my father. He had stayed back to take care of his family. Piya's father was a sand digger.

Piya and I spent a lot of time together. Neither of us went to school. We went, but only for a little while. We stopped early. Piya was going to be a sand digger, like his father. He didn't need any schooling to pick sand from the river. So he dropped out from school; very wise. Piya was always a clever one.

I stopped going to school when the teacher kept me in the same class and my sister Loku and then my brother Jaya passed me and went to a higher class. I knew why that was. The old teacher liked me a lot. He didn't want any other teacher to have me. I told that to my mother. I think my mother was jealous.

'Enough school for you. Better you stay at home.'

She stopped me from going to school.

I didn't mind. I never learnt anything, not even to write my name. I didn't like school at all; too confusing, too many stupid things.

That is how I came to spend a lot of time with my friend Piya.

The other children would go to school and the two of us would have the whole world to ourselves. We would roam everywhere till the sun started going down. That's when we went back home. No point going early. The mothers were tapping rubber and the children were in school. In any case we never had things to eat at midday.

The cooking in our home was simple. My mother cooked in the evening; that we ate in the night. Whatever remained, we ate in the morning. That's how far we went where food was concerned. Nobody complained. My brothers and sisters got a bun in school. The government had made arrangements to give something to eat for the children who came to learn. One reason I didn't mind going to school was that free bun.

I'll tell you all that later. Now it is Piya and I. You see, I must tell his story because he didn't last long.

Piya and I always went about in our motorcars. I enjoyed driving very much. We would drive very fast and take bends as close to the trees as possible, almost touching the tree trunks. Sometimes Piya and I raced our cars. Those races were real fun. We made our track through the coconut trees and then along the slope to the river and along the riverbank. Then we climbed back, struggling on the loose sand. Such times we had to make extra noise with our mouths to show the going was rough. Back into the open we went very fast. That was the last part of the race. We always took turns to win. That way it was always nice. One day it was I who won, the next day it was Piya's turn.

We were both very good drivers, but I think Piya was better than me. He could make all sorts of noises including breaking and tooting the horn. We reversed our cars too. Piya was a champion at reversing. He would struggle with the reverse gear, like the bus drivers did, shake the make believe lever and with difficulty engage the gear. Then he would stand up straight and look behind, turning only his neck. The reversing began - and

Sam's Story

Piya would slow step backwards shuddering his body, just like the buses reversing in the town depot.

Piya was a real good driver. It was great fun driving motorcars with him.

Sometimes we would go and sit by the river and watch the men bring out the sand. Then we would talk. Piya learnt many things from his father about the world. I didn't know anything because I had no father to tell me. So I learnt from Piya. I wanted to tell these things to my brothers and sisters.. You see, they had no father either and I was the eldest and was supposed to take care of them. But by the time I went home, I had forgotten most things. It was useless.

Piya told me that we must always be friends.

'When we grow up I'll dig sand and you can become a driver.'

That was Piya's plan for our future. He was very good at making plans for the two of us. He always made them and I always agreed. He was good.

'You are good with cars, you drive well.'

I liked when he said nice things like that. Piya was the only one who said I was good at something. He also had an idea to join the military. He was the first one who told me about the war in the north and what was happening in the country. He said it was easy for village boys like us to become soldiers.

'The town boys don't like to join the military. They have other jobs.' That's what Piya said.

'The pay is good and even if you die, the government will pay money to the family.'

He knew all these things. I thought it would be a good job to become a soldier. But Piya said that it was not for me. He said we have to kill people. He knew I didn't like that. Neither did he.

He always spoke of the things we would do when we became

men. We made all kinds of plans. It was nice to think of things that could be pleasant and talk of times that would be nice. It was an easy way to be happy; to colour our little world with rainbow dreams. It is a pity Piya is no longer here. Sometimes I wish he would come back.

But even I know he won't.

The Boy

I liked staying in the river house. For one thing, there was too much to eat. We ate anytime and anything we wanted. That's what the Madam told us.

'You must eat,' she used to tell us all the time, as if it was some very difficult thing to do.

So we ate. Even though Leandro was stupid, I must say that he was a better cook than my mother ever was. At least he had things to put in the pots for cooking. We ate three times a day; morning, afternoon and night. What we couldn't finish we put in the icebox and ate later. I must remember to tell you about the ice boxes in the river house.

You see, I have so many stories that I don't know where to begin and where to end.

My days in the river house were of three different kinds. I named them myself. There were lazy days, busy days and enjoyable very busy days. It was simple to separate. It had to do with the people who lived there. Lazy days were when the Master, Madam and their children were away; just Leandro, Janet and me and Harrison for the nights. Nothing much happened in the house. It was lazy. We did our jobs; Leandro did his stupid cooking, Janet made and remade the beds, for what reason I do not know. Nobody slept in them. I swept the garden. That wasn't stupid because whether the Master was there or not the leaves always fell. The days crawled slowly as there was little work to do.

For me I did not like the lazy days. I had nobody to talk to. The other two always spoke in their language. They laughed a lot too, especially when nobody was at home. Not real laughing, but more like chicken laughs - small and long, soft and cackling, just silly, like chicken.

I never joined them and their stupid laughs. I spent time with Bhurus and Lena. The three of us would go to the river end and sit on the grass and watch the river. It was nice, especially in the evenings before the sun went down. The fish would jump; the cormorants would fly down and land on the water, the parrots flew overhead, going to their far-away homes. The sky was always full of birds. The river boats would go past our house, rowed sluggishly by the bare-bodied fishermen. They would be on their way upriver to fish for the night. They all knew me. The fishermen always waved when they saw me sitting in the garden with Lena and Bhurus. Sometimes they even called me to go with them.

I would wait by the river till the sun disappeared and then go back to the house to switch on the lights. That's how the day went - lazy.

Then Harrison would come and the chicken laughs would stop.

When Harrison was there Leandro became quiet as a mouse. No more laughing, no more democratic votes and such things. It was Harrison who decided what to watch on the television. He always watched English things as if he could understand them. Nobody dared to ask him. We were all a little afraid of Harrison. When Master and Madam were not at home, he was the 'Boss'. He made the rules for the three of us, Janet, Leandro and me.

I did not like lazy days; too quiet, nothing happened.

You see, my Master was also a driver like Harrison. My Master himself told me that. He didn't drive cars, but big aerobblanes in

Sam's Story

the sky. He said that is why everybody called him Captain. He once showed me a picture of him and his aerobblane. It was big. He said about four hundred people went in that. That must be a lot; by the way he sounded, it must be a lot. He told me he goes from country to country in his aerobblane taking people and dropping people. He explained many things, but I cannot remember. All I know is that he is a driver and goes to other countries and Madam also sometimes goes with him.

Now you understand what I meant. How my lazy days came about.

The busy days were when Madam and Master were home. They had many friends and the friends always visited and came to eat and drink in our river house. At such times, nothing was quiet. There was a lot of noise and laughing. Not chicken laughs, but real laughs. The evenings became very busy. The gate alone took a lot of my time, to open when the cars came and to close when the cars went.

I had another special job. I was the only one who could do it. My Boss never trusted Janet or Leandro. It was the bar job. I was the barman, that's what the Boss called me. I was the one who made the drinks for the visitors. The Boss himself taught me the bottles. I knew them by the colours. Master always drank the one he called Russian.

'Sammy makes the best drink, perfect measures,' he always boasted to his friends. 'He is an expert.'

I was indeed an expert. Everybody who drank my Russian said my drinks were the best. They loved the way I made it. Most evenings when there were visitors my Master and Madam would sit with them in the big room facing the river. Then my Master would shout 'Sam, Russian!' That is all. I knew exactly what bottle to take and how much to put and how to add tonic and ice. I even cut my own slice of lemon to put to swim in it.

Most visitors who came to the river house drank what my Master drank - Russian. Some would ask for other things, we had them all. I didn't know much about the other bottles, but I knew beer. That is simple. Even Leandro could do it. Open the can and pour into a big glass. You didn't have to be an expert to serve beer. A lot of people asked for is-scotch. They said it in a funny way, but I could never do that. My Boss tried hard to teach me how to say it and he failed. To me it was always is-scotch. That I served with soda or water, but always with ice.

Serving the drinks was no problem. The thing was to watch after serving. My Master taught me that too.

'Sam, as soon as a glass is finished, you have to come fast, like a bat out of hell and take it and fill another one.'

I was very good at it; I mean, this refilling business. The visitors most times said 'no, no, enough,' but they always took it when I came back with the drinks.

I was the best barman. Everybody who came to the river house said so, quick and fast - like a bat out of hell.

The busy days were like that; a lot of people visited the river house, especially in the evenings. They all laughed, drank and ate. Everyone needed me for this and that and I was always there. Time passed very fast when Master and Madam were at home.

The third type, the enjoyable very busy days were when the Boy and the Girl came home. Every year they came to the river house twice. About a month in June and a long time during the year's end. They came by aerobblane from a far away country where they were learning. I liked them both, but I liked the Boy better. There was nothing wrong with the Girl, but she was a bit stupid. Always tried to teach me things, like that Bhurus business. But she was kind.

Sam's Story

The Boy, he was very nice, he was my friend and we did many things together whenever he was at home. That is what made those days enjoyable and very busy.

The Boy often took me when he went in the car, even when he went to Colombo to visit his friends. His friends were also nice. They always joked with me and said things for me to laugh. They were all happy people. I think they were all rich, that's what made them always laugh.

One day my Master's son took me to see a picture; he calls them 'moving.' It was the first time I went to a 'moving'. It was about a boxing man called Rock Man. There was a huge picture of this man pasted outside the hall, red running shorts and no *baniyama,* bare bodied, and his face was covered with blood.

The Boy bought tickets and took me inside a large dim hall. There were not many people, but there were hundreds of chairs, rows and rows, all neatly arranged. We went and sat.

It was quite complicated to sit on these theatre chairs. You have to watch it. I almost made a total fool of myself.

The first time I sat, the seat rolled. I went down, my legs shot up and my poor arse almost slid to the ground. I was stuck between the seat and the back. You see, these seats were funny seats, they go up and down from the front and the back, like a seesaw in a children's park. If you are not careful, you fall. That is what happened to me. I wasn't careful. I just fell. Luckily I managed to hold on to the armrest without going the full distance. The Boy helped me; he pulled me up and saved me.

The people who were seated behind us laughed. I was too busy crawling back to sit right to pay any attention to their stupid laughter. From that moment I made a bad start to this 'moving' business.

Sitting itself was difficult, balancing both sides to keep the seat straight; it took a lot of effort, lot of worry too. After a while I managed to calm myself and sit still. I even did what others were doing, swinging gently up and down. Once the seating problem was solved I was ready for the 'moving'. I must admit that in a small way I was excited.

They made the room very dark and terrible noises came from the roof, very loud. I got frightened. There were large people in front, on the wall; houses, motorcars and even trees and big roads. All this was very new to me, you see, I have never been to a 'moving' before. I was very frightened by the noise and the large giant size of the people who were walking and talking on the front wall.

With all these things happening around me I forgot to balance my seat and nearly fell again. The worst was I couldn't understand anything. People laughed, people ran, cars were going very fast and some went out of the road and fell into the sea.

The boxing man was always there, hitting the air with his hands. Most times he mumbled and spoke as if he was drunk. He looked a bit stupid too. One time he was chasing a small chicken and trying to catch it while his friend an old man kept shouting at him. I think the boxing man was a butcher too. I don't know what kind of a butcher he was. Instead of cutting and selling meat he was running around in an ice room hitting the carcasses with his bare hands and grunting like a pig.

Some butcher.

Many other things happened in the 'moving.' Some people ate other's faces and some ate each other's ears. There were a few who even took off their clothes and slept in beds on top of each other. I think they were doing those things. All this was happening on the wall and I was very confused. But I managed. I simply sat there carefully balancing my chair and watching things I just couldn't understand.

The noise became less after some time and the lights came back.

Sam's Story

It was like the sunrise in the river house. Slowly the darkness went and I could see the other people who were sitting and watching the wall. They were getting up and walking out.

The Boy said it was half time and we too went out of the hall.

People were all moving about in the corridor eating ice cream and potato chips. Some were drinking Coca Cola from bottles and smoking cigarettes. We also bought cone ice creams; one for him and one for me and the two of us stood in a corner eating them. That was when I noticed the women going and coming out of the small room. Men also went and came out, but it was a different room. The Boy said that the rooms were the toilets and they went there to piss, all at the same time. Men had one and women had one, that's how it was.

It reminded me of Piya's father's women only toilet. Maybe he too must have gone to a 'moving' and saw how it was all done and copied the idea. It doesn't matter now. They are no more. I mean, my friend Piya and his sand-digging, toilet-making father.

I didn't go back to the 'moving' after the half time. I told the Boy I didn't want to go back to the dark and the noise. He patted me and said OK and told me to wait near the car till the 'moving' finished. He even gave me some money to eat another ice cream. He was always nice to me, the Boy. That is why I called him my friend.

Anyway, I did not care very much for this 'moving' business. I didn't need any 'movings' in my life. Half of a 'moving' was more than enough to last me a lifetime.

When we were driving back home, the Boy told me not to tell anybody about how I fell from the seat. He also told me to keep quiet about seeing only half a 'moving'.

'They will laugh at us Sam,' he said.

I don't know why he said so, but I didn't want anybody to

laugh at my friend. Till this day, I have not told anybody about my going to half a 'moving' and how I fell from the seat.

We did so many other things too when we were together.

The Boy had a great love to swim and bathe in our river. He called me to join, but I didn't go. I found it a little stupid to bathe in the river when there were so many showers in the house. You see, the thing is, at night I never went to the toilet. I always pissed into the river. I guess it was an old habit. I didn't like to wash from the same water that I pissed into. I didn't want to tell that to the Boy. Even if I told him, I think he still would have been swimming in the river. I didn't want to spoil his fun. The Boy was my friend.

That is how I spent my enjoyably busy days.

I did my daily work, like sweeping the garden and watering the plants. I served Russian drinks, or beer, or whatever anybody wanted. I went in the car with the Boy and I pretended to learn when the Girl tried to teach me English and how to do things properly. She even helped me once to write a letter home.

'You must always keep in touch Sam. If you cannot write, tell me, I'll write for you.'

I don't know what she meant about touch and that. I have never got a letter in my life. I knew nothing about letters, or for that matter anything about writing and reading. Piya and I hardly went to school.

That is why the Girl wrote letters for me.

I told her what to write and she wrote. The letters were only to my mother and my sisters. I included my brothers too. It was better that way. I had nobody else. I didn't want to tell my home people much about the good life. I think it would have made them sad, especially when they had nothing.

Sam's Story

I told the Girl to write and tell my mother to come sometime to visit me in the river house. I told my mother to come with either Loku or Podi. They knew how to go in a bus. I wanted them to see where I lived and what I ate and what I did. I wanted my mother to meet my three friends, Bhurus, Lena and the Boy.

I told her not to come with empty hands but to bring something for the Madam if she came; maybe some eggs.

I never knew whether the letters ever reached my mother or not. Even if they did, I don't know whether she could read. Anyway, I used to wait for days for a reply after the letters went. The Girl said there must always be a reply to a letter. So I waited. They never came. Maybe my mother didn't have money to buy stamps. Anyway, it wasn't important. My letters were about simple things that mattered to me; about how I watered the garden and how I switched the lights and sometimes about my friend Bhurus; nothing important, nothing worth replying to.

Now you know what my enjoyably busy days were like.

It was great when the Boy and the Girl came to the river house for their holidays. In addition to my normal duties like sweeping the garden and watering the plants and attending to the lights, I was so busy doing so many other things and going to so many places. I had no time to think about Leandro and his chicken laughs or his stupid cooking and his stupid democratic voting. When the Boss' children were home, I was mostly with them. Such times I laughed a lot. I was a very happy man.

Come to think of it, it is something new I learnt in the river house; this business of laughing and being happy.

Kaluwa

I cannot honestly remember a single day that someone laughed in my own house. I mean really laughed, with a lot of noise and stomachs shaking, like the people who came to the river house did. We smiled at times. Not too often, but we did smile from time to time. Even when we smiled, they were small smiles. I think the poor can give only small smiles. Since we were poorer than the poor, our smiles were mostly smaller than small smiles. Just appeared and disappeared, like a broken moon in a cloud filled sky.

It is strange, when you think about it, that when you are poor, you cannot even afford something as cheap as a smile. But then, we had a life to live - there were much more important things in it than simply smiling and laughing.

I cannot remember too many things that happened in my childhood. We were there, just growing up in our poor world. That's all. Nothing much took place in our lives. We lived in our house in the village and threw our dirt into the river. My mother tapped rubber and my brothers and sisters went to school. I stayed home and loafed about with my friend Piya. In the evening we all came home and my mother cooked some rice. Sometimes she was too tired; too much tapping rubber, bending and cutting trees the whole day. Then it was my sister Loku who cooked.

We had coupons given by the government to buy rice from the

Sam's Story

co-operative store in town. It was almost free. So we had rice. The rest we ate was mostly pure chance. We only ate vegetables, never meat, not even fish. My mother said we are good Buddhists and good Buddhists only ate vegetables.

'It is what we are taught in our temple. We must never harm the living. We must never eat meat,' she said ever so often. We all knew there was more to it than pure religion.

I didn't mind not eating meat. But my brothers Jaya and Madiya always grumbled. I don't think they wanted to be good Buddhists. They hated eating only vegetables.

Our village had one shop. It was located at the place where our little road met the big road. That's where we stood for buses to go to the town. It was not a shop like the ones in my Master's town. There were no racks filled with things here. There were no cardboard pictures of pretty women smiling with white teeth to sell toothpaste. There was no icebox full of food or glass cases crammed with Maliban biscuits and Kandos chocolate. This shop was definitely not like the ones in my Boss' town. It was a poor people's shop. Only the shop owner was rich.

People who came here to buy things never brushed their teeth with toothpaste and they certainly didn't eat Maliban biscuits or Kandos chocolates. This place only had the small things that we villagers needed. The shop also sold a lot of other people's things; other people's eggs, other people's bananas and other people's vegetables.

The villagers didn't have much money. Almost all of them were rubber tappers and sand diggers. They bought things from this shop and wrote it in a book to pay later. When they had things in their houses like eggs, or in their gardens like bananas and vegetables, they gave it to the shop to reduce what they owed.

That's how the shop came to sell other people's things.
Some of the people in the village even gave their rice coupons.
I know my mother did. That's how she reduced what she had written in the book. She was always in debt to the shop.

The shop was owned by Kaluwa's father. The shop was part of their house. Shop in front and the family lived behind. Kaluwa's name was Siri, but he was always known as Kaluwa. I think it was because he was real black, I mean more like dark blue, almost like a devil's colour. He had the blackest face I have ever seen anywhere. No wonder they all called him Kaluwa.

I don't know Kaluwa's father's real name. Everybody in the village called him *Kade Mudalali*. They all knew that he was a rich man. When I first went to school, Kaluwa also went with me. That's how I came to know him. He was not like Piya; he wasn't nice. He would always talk of the things he ate at home and who came to their house and where he went with his father. I am sure he exaggerated.

Piya and I could never match Kaluwa's talk. Nobody visited our houses, we didn't go anywhere and we never ate anything that was worth talking about. So we lied; both Piya and I. We made up great stories about what we ate and who visited our houses and told them to Kaluwa. I think he knew we were lying. But that didn't stop us. It was great fun to imagine such nice things, to make up stories and tell Kaluwa. It was great for Piya and me to make believe and live a while in those beautiful lies.

Kaluwa would sometimes bring those wrapped sweets from his father's shop and eat them in school. He never gave me any. He used to give me the coloured wrapping paper. No sweets, only paper. I took them home and showed my sisters. I used to lie to them too.

'We had sweets today. The red and white ones that taste like *ice-palam*.'

I felt big telling Loku and Podi the wrappers were from the sweets Kaluwa and I ate.

My sisters always wanted the wrapping paper. The wrappers were nice, blue and green and red and yellow, always in stripes. Loku and Podi would carefully stretch the crumple marks on the wrappers with their fingers and place them inside their books; each wrapper in a different place, to keep them stretched between the pages. God knows for what?

Maybe they had learnt to lie too. Maybe they showed the papers to their friends and told them they also ate red sweets that tasted like *ice-palam.*

I guess when you are poor it is all right to lie. That's the only way you can get others to notice you and make you feel important.

We had four hens. I don't know from where we got them, but I know they were ours. They just walked about and picked things from the ground to eat. They came back in the evening like us and slept in the large cardboard box that my little brother made into a chicken coop. The chicken always laid their eggs there. We never ate eggs.

'Good Buddhists cannot eat eggs.'

That's what my mother always said and sold the eggs to *Kade Mudalali.* He never gave us any money. It was only to reduce my mother's debts. We bought our kerosene oil, sugar, tea leaves and some other things like small soap pieces and boxes of matches from Kaluwa's father. We were always in debt like all the other villagers. Everything was written in the book. When my mother got money for tapping rubber, she gave most of it to *Kade Mudalali.* I don't think he was a nice man. Many times I heard him shout at my mother asking for more money. He cursed her for always being in debt.

Money was the big thing with *Kade Mudalali*. We never had any money. Maybe that's why he scolded my mother so often. We must have been pretty small to him.

That is how we managed to live. A one roomed cadjan house by the river, a little money earned by my mother tapping rubber, coupon rice from the cooperative and the rest of the things from *Kade Mudalali*. We always ate *gotukola* and *kankun* that grew wild on the riverbank. It was free. That was what we had with our rice at most times, *gotukola* and *kankun*.

Vegetables and rice, like good Buddhists.

Our house always woke up early. It was the chickens who woke us. They started their chicken laughs even before the sun rose. Our chickens were much better than the alarm watches we had in the river house. Every night Janet had to wind them and set the time for the watches to ring for us to get up in the morning. Back at home it was different. The chickens needed no winding or setting any time. They always woke early and gave their chicken laughs to wake us.

My mother went to tap rubber at first light and my brothers and sisters had to go to school. I had nothing to do, but I also woke up early to do nothing.

It wasn't often that we had things to eat in the morning, but we had tea; plain hot tea with sugar. My little sister Podi is the one who made the tea and sometimes she was quite generous with the sugar. We loved it, but my mother always scolded her for wasting too much sugar.

I think everything that happened in our house, even simple things like how much sugar went into our tea, was directly connected to the *Kade Mudalali* and his debt book. My mother always said so. He scolded her when the debts were large and she scolded us for wasting too much sugar.

Sam's Story

I think it was all about money. I mean, not having enough of it. That was life for us at home; at least some of the things that happened. There were many more, but none of them are nice to remember. They were mostly no money stories, always reminding us how poor we were.

So how to smile, let alone laugh?

Leandro

Apart from the days being lazy, there were other reasons why I didn't like when the Master and Madam went way. These were big bad reasons.

As soon as the Master and Madam left, Leandro always started his stupid war talk, this Eelam and tiger business. It was about the war where his people were fighting my people and about cutting the country into two and such things. I didn't know enough to talk back to him. Leandro knew everything. He knew who died and where the bombs exploded. He knew how many died and who shot whom and why. He even knew who was going to die. I mean which one among our leaders was going to be killed.

Leandro always listened to the radio and watched television. He got very excited whenever there was something about the war. He would listen to the news carefully and then come running to taunt me.

'Enough for you?' He would make violent faces and hiss at me through clenched teeth.

'Another hundred of your bastards gone.'

Leandro would strut about his kitchen like a peacock and relate the news stories with pride, as if he himself had killed the hundred. I just kept quiet. Then he would run and tell Janet. It always ended with Leandro giving his chicken laugh.

Sam's Story

I knew there was a war. I knew it was between Leandro's people and my people. But I didn't know really why they fought and killed each other. My Boss didn't know either. He always said it was all very meaningless.

'I want no part of it,' he would tell all his friends when they spoke about it. 'That war is purely political, to fulfill the empty ambitions of our leaders,' he would explain. 'It is a war for the rich to get more rich and for the poor to die.'

That was my Boss' simple explanation of the war that was going on in the north.

His friends too agreed about the stupidity of the war. To me it was confusing. I knew people died in a war, but I could never figure out how people got rich.

Nobody seemed to know what the war was really about except Leandro. He told me that very soon his people would come to Colombo and take over the government. He said our people were stupid. They didn't know how to fight a war. He said in their army everyone fought, including the leaders. In ours, he said, only the poor people fought.

'Your army, only poor people's sons become soldiers,' he would educate me, as if I didn't know. 'The rich people's sons play cricket.' He had theories like this.

'Your people,' Leandro's eyes would go on fire and he would point his index finger at me and yell, 'only willing to kill.'

'Our people,' he would beat his hand on his chest like an upturned turtle and shout, 'we are willing to die.'

'That is why we will win,' he would give the final verdict.

The last part was always in a whisper, I mean, the winning part. It was as if he, Leandro, the stupid cook, was the one who decided who won and who lost this war. I could never make head or tail of what he said. I guess it was just like the war. I just couldn't understand.

I think my Master was right. It was all meaningless.

Leandro often brought his gods into our war arguments. You see, Leandro and I shared the room outside the main house. 'Your living quarters,' that's what the Madam said. We had all our things there, our clothes and the little other pitiful things that we called ours in the world. We had our gods too; one for me and some for him, framed in cheap wood and hanging on the wall that was full of nails and nail holes. I had a faded picture of the Buddha and Leandro had his gods in bright coloured pictures; some with many hands which carried spears and swords and some who looked like giants. He always prayed to his gods and lit sandalwood joss sticks in the evening.

I must admit, that in a way, my God was neglected. I never prayed nor offered incense.

Leandro would always tell me that his gods were powerful and all his people prayed to them to win the war. He said his gods were much more powerful than my God. That is why he was sure they would win the war.

'Look at yours,' he would point at the picture in the wall and speak in a ridiculing tone. 'Hands are folded, legs are folded, and eyes are closed.' He would close his eyes and fold his hands in mimic imitation. 'Too timid,' that was the conclusion.

'Look at mine,' he would then point to his gods. At such times he would stand on his toes to be tall and expand his chest like a bullfrog, just to depict strength. 'Very powerful, very big, many hands, many weapons, and eyes wide open.' He would then nod his head and ask, 'You see what I mean?'

'Who do you think is more powerful?' The question was direct.

'Yours or mine?'

I did see what he meant. Even though I never said anything, I

Sam's Story

must admit this god business frightened me. That was one reason I was a little scared of Leandro. He prayed everyday and I knew his gods were powerful. He was right. Mine looked a bit timid. That worried me.

The war talk always increased whenever Velu came to the river house. Velu was also their kind. He worked for my Master's friend, Mr. Gunasekera. They lived on the next lane where you turned near the water tap. After Leandro, the one I disliked most was Velu. He never spoke to me, only to Leandro and Janet. He would come to the river house with messages from his master to my Master. They were always written messages. He never gave them to me. Always wanted to come inside the house and give the letters himself. Velu was a slimy one. He would bend in two when he spoke to my Master, as if his spine was about to break.

Whenever Velu came to give his messages, he would end up in the kitchen to chat with Leandro. Sometimes Janet too joined them. They only talked in their language. Sometimes Velu would open the icebox and eat. I didn't like that, but it was Leandro's kitchen. I had no say in that matter.

Velu and Leandro always spoke in whispers, like love-makers. I knew they were speaking of the war. Leandro's chicken laughs would start and go on till Velu left.

I think Velu knew more about the war than Leandro. His master and madam worked in Colombo and they knew more things. He learnt from them and came to tell Leandro about what was happening. As soon as he left, I got the full dose from Leandro, maybe exaggerated. It was always about the war, how stupid our people were, specially our leaders and how clever their people had become in fighting this war.

Janet seldom said anything about this war talk. That way she was nice. She once told me that she did not like the war or what was happening in the north. She said her younger brother had been missing for many years because of the fighting.

'He was only a small boy, Sam, they came and took him away,' she told me.

I didn't know that people got lost in wars.

She said she does not like to talk about it.

'Too sad, Sam,' she sighed.

I knew what she meant. I felt the same way whenever I remembered the ones I lost. It was something I couldn't talk about. My mother had made me promise never to speak about the war. My little brother Madiya wanted it that way. But I told Janet about Piya. I told her how he got lost when the river overflowed and how he died and how the fish ate him before we found his body.

Maybe Janet's brother is also dead.

When people are lost, I think they die. That is why she is sad and does not want to talk about the war.

Leandro always said that one day he would go and join his army. He said that he cooked now because his family had no place to stay and he wanted to make a house for his mother and sister.

'Once the house is built, no more cooking, I am gone' he made his promises. I think he wanted to be big in Janet's eyes. That is why he came out with this soldier talk. He was so short that they would not even see him if he went to fight.

'I know where to go and I know what to do and the first bastard I will kill when I become a soldier is you,' he said half-mockingly nodding his head like a cow. I knew that the other half was true. He meant it.

That's how much Leandro hated me. I think this war had spilt way beyond the leaders who were planning and the soldiers who were fighting. It had even made stupid cooks like Leandro hate stupid gardeners like me. It was a matter of what kind you

Sam's Story

belonged to - you always hated the other kind; like Leandro hating me and me hating Velu, all because someone else was fighting a war to divide the country in two.

All this fighting and hatred that we had in the river house was about something that we hardly knew anything about.

My Master was like me; he was no fool. He saw things simple and had real answers for anything that needed answers. He was always busy, going here, going there, people coming to meet him, him going to meet people. Always busy.

In the morning when he came down from his room upstairs to start the day he would go at me like a machine gun.

'Sam, how's life?'

Before I could reply he would continue.

'No problems? Good.'

He asked, he answered and he concluded, all by himself. Then he would be gone. He was always that busy. I had time only to grin when he asked these questions. So I grinned.

This was a ritual every morning when he was home. As he saw me, I think he got ready with his lines and I was ready for him with my grin.

Sometimes when I was in the garden he would come and talk to me. There was a big pond in our garden with a statue of a naked boy pissing into the pond. My Master's brother made that statue boy. The brother is an art man. The statue boy's piss wasn't real piss; it was only water. Harrison's friend Lionel the plumber had done the fixing for the piss. A pipe came from underground, passed through a small motor and joined to the thing of the naked boy. That's how he pissed fresh water. There was a switch hidden among the rocks that were scattered around the pond. You switched it on, the motor started and the boy pissed.

I don't know why my Master, Harrison and Lionel went into all that trouble to get this naked statue boy to piss water from his cement thing. I could have done it everyday without any problem, real thing and real piss. No need to have pipes and hide switches and have motors running.

It could have been very simple.

We had a lot of fish in the pond, all colours and all sizes. It was my Master's pond and they were his fish. My Master liked feeding the fish. But I don't know why he needed a pond to feed fish when the big river was just there with so many fish to feed. I asked him that and he laughed.

'Good question Sammy, good question.' That's all he said. Never gave me the answer.

We had these green balls kept in an old Horlicks bottle. That was fish food. Harrison bought them at a fish shop in town. We just threw the little balls; a handful in the pond and the fish jumped all over and fought each other to eat them.

That was what my Master liked to watch.

I had two important jobs to do where the pond and the fish were concerned. First, I had to keep the pond clean and then I had to feed the fish. Very clear instructions that came directly from the Boss himself.

There were many large trees in our garden and many leaves fell. The ones that fell on the ground, I swept. The ones that fell into the pond I took out. I had to carefully take them out one by one. That was simple. The whole idea was to keep the pond clean and I made sure every leaf that fell was taken out.

The other job was even simpler. Taking the green balls from the Horlicks bottle and throwing them in the pond for the fish to eat.

Sam's Story

'Sam, you must feed them every six hours.'

That's what the Boss told me. Now there was a problem.

I was not very good at this time business. Back in the village we never bothered about time. We had no clock, only the chicken to wake us up. The rest of the day and what we did had its own pace; never by time. That is why this business of every six hours to feed the fish was a bit complicated.

But as I said before, my Master was no fool. He saw my problem and he quickly found an answer.

'Sam, don't worry about six hours,' he helped me out. 'Every time you eat, you go and feed the fish.'

Now that is what I call clever; a simple solution to a seemingly complicated situation.

My problems with feeding the fish were over.

I ate bread for breakfast; the fish ate their green balls. I ate rice for lunch; they had green balls. Whatever and whenever I ate, the fish got their share of green balls. They always fought each other and jumped about in the pond to eat their green balls. I sometimes felt bad that I ate so many different things and the fish only had green balls for every meal.

I told that to my Master. He said not to worry.

'Sam, the fish are not like people, they are not fussy and they don't grumble. They are easy to satisfy, they wouldn't mind.'

That's what he said to settle me.

Sometimes my Master took me in his car. I enjoyed going about with him. His car was a big dark red car with light brown seats. This car was always very clean; the outside was well polished. The inside always smelt nice, like dressed up women. My Master was very fussy about how his car looked and how it smelt. Every time the car went out and came, Harrison and I washed and cleaned it. I think I washed that car more times than I washed my own face.

I will never forget the first trip I made in my Master's car. As soon as we sat and the Boss started the engine, it began to get very cold. The inside of the car became like an icebox, like the one in Leandro's kitchen; almost unbearable. I shivered and suffered and pretended that it was nice. I was wearing a *baniyama* with no sleeves; more like bare-bodied and the cold was unbearable. But I managed to shut my mouth and grin like a fool, pretending it was nice to be cold.

That was the only time I got caught. After that I made sure I wore something thick underneath and a shirt on top whenever I went in that icebox car.

The other thing I didn't like about my Master's car was the radio. It played songs without words. That part I couldn't understand. The tunes were also a bit confusing. It went loud and soft, fast and slow, all without anybody singing anything. I asked Janet why it was so and she told me that it is the best music.

'It is classic music Sam,' she said something like that. "No words, no language, nothing for people to fight about.'

That's how Janet explained. Come to think of it, it is true. After that I didn't mind this wordless no fighting music.

The Boss always took me when he went to get his hair cut. We always cut our hair together, he first and me second. The barber shop was in town. It was on top of a place where they sold vegetables, that was Tee Malli's vegetable shop. Tee Malli was a vegetable man who sat behind a stall full of carrots, beetroots and capsicums and all kinds of other vegetables. You name it, he had it, if not fresh, at least in half rotten form. As the vegetables rotted the price came down. That's when the poor bought vegetables.

Tee Malli had to sit on a very tall stool to be seen. He was a very short man, flat head and stunted, as if someone had hit him

Sam's Story

with a giant hammer. He was even shorter than our dwarf Leandro. It was from Tee Malli that Harrison bought all the vegetables for the river house. We were rich; we bought only the very fresh ones.

The hair cutting man was a young boy. He was called Lucky. I think that was his name. I don't know how they can call him Lucky. I never could see any luck in him. He didn't even have a pair of slippers to wear. Always stood on bare feet to cut hair.

Lucky's barber shop was nothing much either, just two chairs and a wooden bench to sit on, with one mirror that needed a bit of cleaning. The shop was noisy too, very noisy. All the street noises blasted into Lucky's shop from the open window - cars blaring their horns, lorries and buses revving engines in blocked traffic and Tee Malli shouting at the top of his voice to get people to buy his vegetables.

Lucky also added his contribution to the shop noise with his tape radio. It was always on. He only had two tapes, one Hindi and one Baila, which he played over and over again. When the Hindi finished, he would change to Baila and go back to Hindi at the end of the Baila.

That was all right, come to think of it, two tapes was all he needed. There weren't many people who came to Lucky's barbershop to get their hair cut. The waiting was never long enough to last two tapes.

Every time I went there the same music played. Lucky's customers were forced to listen to his Hindi-Baila concert. The tapes were just like his half- torn old magazines and his red and white striped window curtains. They never changed. When my Master was getting his hair cut, I sat on the bench and listened to the same songs and looked at the same pictures in the same old magazines. I always thought how dirty the not so white stripes in his permanent curtains had become.

There were steps that led from the vegetable shop at the bottom to Lucky's barbershop. That's how you had to come to get your hair cut. These steps were half steps, small size, like a poor man's steps. You had to climb them keeping the feet sideways. The steps to Lucky's shop were the same as his curtains, always dirty, always covered with hair, blobs of mixed grey and black that had been swept from the shop floor above.

Every time I went up those hairy steps into Lucky's barber shop and sat near the dirty window curtains, looked at Lucky with no shoes cutting my Master's hair and blocked my ears to the Hindi Baila mixing with the blaring street noises, I knew that there really wasn't too much luck in this Lucky.

The barber knew my Boss well. My Master did not have to tell Lucky how to cut and things like that. He just sat in the chair and Lucky knew exactly what to do. The cutting would begin and Lucky would start his detailed report about everyone and everything that happened in the town, from the last haircut to this one.

'He is also my news man Sam, the best there is,' my Master would tell me whenever we stopped the car for the haircut. 'That's why I always come to him to get my hair cut.'

'Let's go and listen to the town update,' he said every time when we climbed sideways those half-sized dirty steps.

Lucky knew everything that happened in town; who died and got buried and who and how many came for the funeral. He knew who fought whom and went to the police and who said stories about whom and which ones were lies and which ones were the truth. He knew who left our town and went away to far places to work. He always mentioned some place called Dubai. He himself wanted to go there to cut hair.

Sam's Story

Lucky also knew all the love stories that took place in our town; who married whom, stuff like that. He told them all to my Master whilst he sat in the barber's chair. Lucky whispered some things too; I think they were mainly vulgar things concerning rogue lovers. About other peoples wives and who quietly took them during day time to the rooms in the *'vinodai visvasai'* guesthouses when the husbands were away at work. Those whispers were always on stories like that. Such stories must have had happy endings. Most times my Master and Lucky laughed when the whispering was over. It was always a bit of a naughty laugh.

Whenever there were cricket matches, Lucky only spoke of cricket. I think this Lucky was a big cricket man and got very excited when he spoke of cricket. He knew all the names of the players and what happened in matches and wanted to know everything else that was happening. Who played whom and how much they scored, that kind of stuff, all the details of the cricket matches.

He was also an expert on other things in cricket, like who should be the captain of our team and which umpire cheated and why someone was taken and why someone was dropped. That's how he said it. So many 'whys'.

He would pester my Master to comment on his cricket theories and was very happy whenever my Boss agreed with his expert opinions.

Sometimes he would talk about the government too.
He would always sound angry whenever he spoke of the government and the people who ran our country.

Again the barber's 'whys' would come, for which my Master was always silent.

Why this? And, why that? Lucky went on all on his own, voicing his many 'whys' about what was happening in the country.

My Master only nodded. The barber most certainly had too many whys about the people who were ruling us and what they did to the country. I don't think any of these government 'whys' had any answers.

But like a fool, he kept asking them.

No answers, only questions.

My Master knew everybody in town. He knew the man in the petrol shed where we went to pump petrol and service the car. He knew Lucky the barber. Menda, the man in the bakery where we bought bread and buns was also his friend. Menda was a muscle man, a bit of a *Thadha Banda,* always with his hair cut short and always wearing very tight tee shirts to show his big muscles. Then there was Ranjith, the one who ran the shop called Doltans near the traffic lights. That shop had everything.

So many others in town were my Master's friends. They were all known to him or I think it was more like he was known to them. He would stop the car and send me to get things. He never got out. Always stayed in the car, icebox cold, listening to his wordless music.

Sometimes we would meet some friend of his and he would introduce me.

'This is our new addition to the house, my new *golaya,*' he would laugh and say to whoever we met. I didn't much like the new addition business, like a piece of furniture or something. But I knew he meant well. That is why he called me his *golaya.*

One day he scolded me. I think that was the only time my Master and I had a fight. It was for something stupid, very stupid. I had forgotten to switch off the lights in the morning and my Master saw the lights shining bright when he came down for breakfast. I think he had got up in a bad mood, maybe even from the wrong side of the bed.

Sam's Story

He asked me whether I was mad.

'It costs money, you fool,' he shouted. 'I have to pay the light bills.'

He shouted many things. I didn't like being called a fool. He knew I was no damn fool. In any case he never paid the bills. It was always Harrison who paid all the bills in the river house.

'You don't pay the bills,' I muttered softly but loud enough for him to hear. 'Harrison is the one who pays them all' I made it clear to him.

For that he really got mad.

'Harrison pays the bills? But it is my money you stupid idiot,' he screamed. 'Harrison pays the bills – my arse' he made his face also like an angry arse and went on shouting like a mad man.

I thought he would hit me. He kept yelling so many things at one time, calling me all sorts of names. He called me a monkey and then a dog and finished the animal list by adding dumb donkey. He was shouting so much that I couldn't even follow what he was saying. Maybe he didn't either. He was so angry. I am sure he must have been angry for something else and took it on the stupid lights and me. His shouting was so loud, so fast and so confusing.

'Don't ever talk back to me, you dumb bastard, I'll cut your balls off and throw it into the pond to feed the fish,' he threatened and screamed again, same angry arse face.

This went on for a while, my Boss yelling at the top of his voice. I stood frozen, too scared to move. Luckily the Madam heard the shouting and came running. She, in her usual calmness, dragged her husband away. He was still screaming meaningless things at me even whilst retreating.

All for some stupid light that I forgot to switch off and for reminding him that it was Harrison who paid the bills.

I didn't take all that shit without giving back. First I was scared, then, I got angry. It was all too much. Master or no Master he had no right to talk to me like that. Call me stupid animal names and about cutting my one and only thing to feed his stupid fish. I was angry and I was definitely not going to let him get away with all that.

I went near the river and sat on the bench under the mango tree.

There I started yelling at him. I knew some choice words too. I called him a dog and a donkey and a pig and I added my own special things. I lifted his sarong and poked a large pineapple up his arse and I made him take his toothbrush and brush his teeth with my shit. I also called him a fool. Not an ordinary fool, but a *val peretha* fool. Worse than what he called me.

I kept shouting for more than ten minutes; much longer than he shouted at me. I was angry. I shouted till my breath ran out. I only stopped when my mouth ran dry and there was no breath left in me to continue my abuse.

So we became even. He shouted at me and I shouted at him. He just shouted at me for no reason, simply because he got up in a bad mood and needed someone to take his anger off.

At least when I shouted, I knew why I did it.

That was the first and the last time. He never got angry with me again nor did I ever shout at him. We quickly became good friends. I think we both realised that shouting was useless and meaningless. This dog and donkey business and calling each other stupid idiot and such names were only empty words.

Anybody can abuse anybody and call anyone anything. For what?

That is how our one and only fight ended, the river house battle between the Big Boss and the Small Boss.

But I must admit that for a long time I carried a few scars of that battle, especially about how he shouted and all the names he called me.

It was more so whenever I threw the green balls to the pond to feed the fish. I used to feel quite scared when I saw them jumping and fighting to eat their food. At those times I would touch my things in protection, just to make sure everything was there.

It took me a long time to get rid of the fearful feeling; the dreadful possibility that I could have ended my days at the river house as Sam the Small Boss without his thing.

Elections

Many interesting things happened in our village in the months before they elected the government leaders. It was a time everybody became excited and forgot all their troubles. It was election time. We all talked only about the new leaders we were going to select and send to the big city to govern us. This is the one time the poor became visible to the rich. We had votes and that mattered.

For once, the poor were becoming important. There was a lot of excitement.

The government election that I'm talking about happened a while before I went to Colombo to work for the white woman, Madam Martell. I don't know how long the 'a while before' was, but this election was definitely before I left for Colombo. That much I clearly remember.

It was a time that we were all at home, Jaya, Madiya, Loku and I. We were just hanging around doing nothing. Podi was still in school and my mother went out in the mornings to tap rubber.

Loku had stopped going to school, so had Jaya and Madiya. The food problem had become even worse at home as the three of them had lost the buns they ate in school. Loku had learnt many things, much more than my brothers did and she was always writing letters to places saying how good she was.

My sister was looking for a job. Sometimes she got replies and sometimes she didn't. Loku always got very excited

Sam's Story

whenever a letter came from a place that she had written to. That excitement was always very short lived.

She never got any job.

Jaya and Madiya of course just loafed about and did what they could. On weekends they went to the town market to carry vegetable boxes from the lorries. Sometimes they got work in the river too. When they needed more men to dig more sand. At such times Jaya and Madiya were called and they went and worked as sometime sand diggers.

They gave some money to my mother. It was very little. They got only a few rupees and even from that they had to smoke *beedi* and drink *kasippu*.

After all the years these three had spent in the school learning so many things, they were no better than the rest of us in the village. Loku just wrote letters and got empty replies. Jaya and Madiya unloaded vegetables in town and sometimes dug sand and got drunk in the evenings.

That was how it was before the election.

There were two people who were important in our village during the election time. One was Kaluwa's father, *Kade Mudalali*, who was the main man for one colour. The other was the one they called *Gurunnanse*, the schoolteacher, who was from the other colour. These two were not the ones who were taking the contest. They were the main supporters of the people taking part - the party bosses for our area. That's what they called themselves. All this was beyond me. These are things I gathered from what I heard. People always talked during election times. Even the quiet ones in the village had something to say.

Every Saturday evening there was a meeting. It was a big event. *Kade Mudalali's* meetings were near his shop and *Gurunnanse's* meetings were always at a clearing that was next to the school.

Luckily they had only one meeting at a time. I think that is the only thing they agreed on. We liked it that way. We didn't want to miss any. You see, we also had votes. That's what the government men who came to our houses to take down our names told us. That's why we went to the meetings, to find out what was happening.

Piya and I were always there at every meeting. We drove in our cars and parked and locked them, in case somebody stole them. Then we went to listen to all the promises they made from the platform.

There were always about five people on the platform at every meeting. They drank Orange Barley from bottles and took turns to speak to us. Both colours had the same kind of meeting and both colours promised the same things.

That was fine with us.

We didn't need to worry about who won and got elected. Either way we would win and get what they promised.

These meetings were rather small and they were supposed to prepare us for the big meeting. That was when the boss-man himself, the one who wanted our votes, came to our village. That meeting was always big, a lot of people, and even the police were there. They always had loud speakers so that everybody could listen to the boss-man's promises.

Both sides had this big day. Both sides wanted our votes. We were all going to get jobs. They were going to give bulb lights to the village and make a playground at the school. These were some of the promises I remember. There were many others. The platforms were full of promises.

They were also saying some things about a garment factory that would be built near our village. That was for the girls who could also then go to work. The factory needed girls to make shirts. The buttons had to be stitched and the packing had to be done. They needed girls. They said the pay would be much more than what people earned tapping rubber or digging sand.

There were so many promises that we simply couldn't wait till the elections were over for the good times to begin. I could even imagine Loku and Podi going to work in a factory and getting money. Maybe they could then buy real sweets from Kaluwa's father. They wouldn't have to pretend they were sweet eaters by hoarding the silly wrapping paper and pressing them inside their books.

As the elections came close we became very important people. *Kade Mudalali* always smiled and never mentioned the debt book. He even came to our house one evening to talk to all of us.

'Make sure you give us the vote and the jobs would be yours,' he promised with all smiles and left to visit Piya's house.

Gurunnanse also came. Said similar things, grinned wide and pretended he was our friend and went away. He also went to Piya's house. I think they both had agreed to do the same things before the elections. *Gurunnanse* and *Kade Mudalali* continuously smiled, made promises to all of us and walked from house to house the same way the other had done.

It was only Piya's father who never got excited about the elections. He always said they were all lies; I mean all these promises about bulb lights and factory jobs and such things. At that time I was sure he didn't know what he was talking about. After all, he was only a sand digger and the only important thing he had done in his life other than digging sand was making a toilet.

What would he know about votes and elections and the promises made by politicians?

The elections finished and *Kade Mudalali's* colour won.

Gurunnanse, our schoolteacher, was punished for being on the other side. That was politics for you. People said he was sent to a far away place, to teach in a Tamil school. No more elections for him. A new teacher, from the *Kade Mudalali's* colour, came to take his place. The bulb lights never came. That was bad. But the worst was when Kaluwa's father raised the price of kerosene. We had to pay more to light our little single wick lamps.

That's how the story of the bright lights coming to our village ended.

It took some time, but the garment factory was built a few miles from our village. It was a big white building with a big garden and there was a high barbed-wire fence all round it. The factory had guards wearing khaki uniforms and caps on their head standing at the gates. That was to stop people from just walking in to this factory. People said the owners were from other lands. They were partners with our *Kade Mudalali's* government. That's what people said. Sometimes we would see these owners driving around in their jeeps. Short white men with flat faces and small eyes.

They needed girls to work in their factory and my mother was very happy to go there and get a form paper. We had to fill it up for Loku to get a job.

'Only one job for one family,' that is what the man in the factory office said. 'We must be fair.'

Loku never got any job. There were too many girls from the area trying to get work in the factory. My mother went with Loku to meet *Kade Mudalali* and pleaded with him. She swore by all the gods she knew that her entire family voted for *Kade Mudalali's* colour.

'How do we know?' that's what he asked.

We never got any job, or bulb lights, or a playground. We got nothing; only promises that vanished like the moonbeams.

Sam's Story

Before they disappeared, they drenched us, soaked us to the skin with happy expectations that turned out to be sad nothings. I think that's what the elections were all about. Colours and meetings and poor people like us given importance till matters were settled.

Then we were all discarded as the dirt we threw into our river. Piya's father was right. Those promises were all lies.

The river overflowed that year. It was sometime after the elections.

Our river was also doing its best to batter us, as if we didn't have enough troubles already. The rains came everyday. It never stopped. It rained and rained and rained. First the river flowed fast, then it started rising. That is when we all left our homes and went away. The water level rose to almost our waist. We had no place to go, nothing to eat and no place to escape from the rain; it was not only us, almost everybody who lived on the riverbank suffered the same way. They all had to leave. The river was rising fast and flowing even faster.

All the people who left their homes went to the village school. Nobody called us; we simply went. There was no other place to go to escape from the rain and the river.

The school building had a roof but the sides were open. The rain blew from the sides and made the floor damp. But that was all right. The building was on high ground; at least the river didn't reach us. We all found our own corners and huddled and stayed, cold from both the rain and the hunger. Children cried and the women cried too. The men stared at the sky in silent anger. They knew the river was rising. They knew what that meant.

When night fell it became more miserable. Two men left to walk in the rain to the main road. They wanted to get to town and get some help. We were all hoping they would come back soon. The wait was long; no one came.

There was no food, no dry clothes, nothing warm to take away the dampness. Someone had two candles and they lit them. For a while it was nice, the little candles glowing in the dark. It was very difficult to keep the flames going. The wind was so strong. The flames blew off in no time and they were lit again. Soon the matchbox finished. The candles were there, no more matchsticks, no way to light. The candles were useless, just like us.

It was the longest night that I can remember.

The next day some people came. I think they were from the town. They came in a van in the pouring rain and got off with umbrellas. These people were from the temple; even the *sadhu* was there.

They knew that the river was overflowing and had heard there were people like us who were homeless and helpless. These people brought bread and bananas for us to eat. It was a feast. We had been so hungry. They left more bread behind for us to eat later. The bananas were over, but there was bread.

The *sadhu* promised to return the next day with more things for us. We pleaded with them to come back. We were helpless.

The rain never stopped.

It was on the second day that Piya and his father left the school building and went to get some things from their house. The water level was high. Though it didn't reach the building in the yard, it was waist high. People told them not to go. But I think they were desperate. Desperate men do desperate things. That's why they went, saying they would try to save some things that were in their house before the river took everything away.

They never came back, they got lost in the water.

Piya's mother and sister lost everything. They lost their men too. The river took them away. It was days later, when the rain had stopped and the water was less, that they found Piya. He was wedged to a branch of a tree in the riverbank. Even after all these years I find it sad to talk about it. I don't like repeating that story. It is too sad.

That's how I lost my friend Piya.

Piya and his father died at the same time. The river overflowed and took away all our things. It took Piya and his father too, along with the toilet they made for their women.

If I remember right, that is the only time I cried. Piya was my friend. He was my best friend before I met Bhurus. Piya was more ugly than Bhurus when they buried him. That is why I cried. The fish had eaten him. They never found his father or the toilet that he built for his women.

By the time the river went back to normal we had nothing left. Our house was there, only the roof and part of the sides. Nothing else. The only ones that escaped the river were our chickens. They had climbed the roof and hopped onto the mango tree.

All we had now was a roof, half a side of the house, and four chickens to begin life again.

Even for poor people like us, it was nothing.

Christmas

Bhurus got sick one morning and started to vomit everywhere. I think he had eaten something wrong. I got scared. Madam took one look at him and yelled for Harrison.

'Harrison please take him; take him in the van to the doctor. Go to Doctor Wijewardena, quickly, hurry up,' she gave all the instructions in one breath. That's how she spoke when something excited her.

Harrison and I loaded Bhurus into the van and took him to Doctor Wijewardena, the dog doctor. When we arrived at the doctor's house, he was already waiting for us at the gate. Our Madam had telephoned.

We all carried Bhurus inside the room and put him on top of a metal table. I have never been to a dog doctor's house, for that matter to any doctor's house. I have only gone to a hospital.

Things were different here. I was surprised to see the fuss they were all making for our Bhurus. I was happy for my friend; he was getting all the attention. Even the doctor's wife came to see him. I think she was our Madam's friend. She was a Muslim madam. I've seen her come to the river house with bowls of sweet *watalappan* whenever they celebrated something.

I kept holding Bhurus till they all looked at him. I kept patting him to keep him calm; I knew he was scared by the way he rolled his big eyes.

Sam's Story

The dog doctor gave him an injection.

'Just a small problemmmm, we'll take care of thhhhat' the doctor added a musical 'hummmm' and almost sang the words in a tuneless song whilst looking at Bhurus' whole body. He started from Bhurus' mouth and went even to his those parts.

'Nothingggg to worrrrryyyy, smmmalll prroblllemmm,' he sang again.

We all waited awhile for Bhurus to settle down.

'Better call and tell your friend,' that's what Doctor Wijewardena told his *watalappan* wife.

This time he didn't sing his silly song; there was no music. The tune was only for Bhurus. 'Call and tell her not to worry. He is all right now, just some food poisoning.'

Watalappan ran to call my Madam to give the good news. Everything was under control.

Bhurus was very lucky that he was a rich dog. He got all the attention.

Doctor Wijewardena gave some more medicine for Bhurus, some pills and some to drink and told us to bring him again the next day.

Harrison asked how much the bill was. The doctor gave him a funny look with eyes wide open.

'Bill, what bill?' he appeared confused.

'No, no, no,' he went on, gesturing the negative with his hands, his mouth, his face and even his legs, like a thief defending himself after being caught for stealing.

'No no, no,' he repeated again. 'No bill for treating your Master's dog, what nonsense.'

The way he said it I got the feeling that it was as if my Master had done him a big favour by getting Bhurus sick and sending the dog to him for treatment.

If he didn't want the money, well that was his problem. I didn't mind that. But I wanted to object to his idea of whose dog it was.

Bhurus was not my Master's dog; he was my dog. My Master only owned him.

'You must look after him carefully,' the doctor told me in a very serious tone. 'You must make sure he takes his medicine.'

I grinned. That was the best answer to these stupid people. Stay silent and grin, it could mean anything and everything. They can take it anyway they want.

Bhurus was my friend. I did not need a dog doctor married to a *watalappan* to tell me how to take good care of him.

The grin was also for the comedy of it all; the fuss they all made for the sick dog. I wondered if I fell ill and came to doctor Wijewardena whether he would treat me the same and sing his tuneless song.

I doubt.

We took Bhurus home. He was quiet; the injection had made him feel drowsy. I had to carry him from the van. He had to take his medicine at the right time, that's what the doctor said. It was I who fed him his pills three times a day and that was not easy. Bhurus didn't like the pills. He was sick and luckily he was too weak to protest. That made it easy for me. In any case I would have made sure he took the medicine.

I didn't want him to be sick. I wanted him to get well and be normal to walk with me in the garden. I wanted him to sit with me by the river and watch the boats go by. He was my friend. I took good care of him.

That evening we had people who came to the river house specially to see Bhurus.

Sam's Story

Mr. Gunasekera's wife was the first to come. As soon as she returned home from office, she came to see Bhurus. I think my Madam must have telephoned and told her about our new patient.

'You must come and visit the sick, no?' That's what she said, patting Bhurus' head. Mrs. Gunasekera was the one who always greeted our Bhurus with her 'Good mornings' and 'Good evenings' on normal days. She was a great dog lover. Our Bhurus was one of her favourites.

There were others who came too, when they heard about Bhurus and his visit to the doctor. Some others called, just to find out whether he was all right.

I don't think Bhurus ever got so much attention in his whole life. My Master's brother came on his motorcycle with his wife and so did my Master's sister with her son. Madam's brother came all the way from Colombo. Hemi Sir came and went straight to the dog and as usual became very serious, closed his eyes and said some things to his God to cure our Bhurus. He was a big prayer man, always talking to his God for everything. Buddy Sir and Shanthi Sir came too. They both had dogs and knew something about why dogs fell sick and things like that. They gave their expert opinion to which we all nodded.

In fact everyone who came to see Bhurus had something to say about why he fell ill. All these visitors seemed to know a lot about dog sicknesses. I wondered with all these experts around why my Madam needed a dog doctor.

Raji Sir was working late and he came almost at midnight. But he was there in time to mark his presence for the event of the day.

It was the first time I realized that in houses like our river house, the dogs had people who came to see them when they fell sick and even had people praying to gods to make them better.

It took almost a week for Bhurus to fully recover. I spent a lot of time with him, seated on the floor, patting his head and giving him all the love he needed. I took good care of him, making sure he took his pills exactly the way doctor Wijewardena wanted. In a few days time he became the normal stupid Bhurus and started wagging his stump of a tail and growling with love whenever he saw me. I was glad. I didn't like it when Bhurus fell sick. I was even worried that something might happen to him. I didn't want to lose him. After Piya, Bhurus was the only real friend I had in the whole world.

Bhurus was lucky he was a rich dog. He got the best possible attention. The van was there to take him to the doctor. Harrison was there to drive and I was there to carry him. What more can a stupid dog like Bhurus expect? The medicine too was free. The dog doctor even sang his tuneless song to Bhurus when he examined him and checked his those things. People came to see him because he was sick. I think people came more to please my Master and Madam. They knew that my Master and Madam would be pleased that their friends took the trouble to come and see their dog.

There was only one thing missing. It was the postman bringing a get better card for Bhurus, like the ones that came for Madam and Master whenever they got a cold.

Life was never like that for us, the poor people. Back home in our village, it was very difficult when anybody got sick. That is why so many died so young. There were no vans to go and no Harrisons to drive; no one to carry us to the doctors. No one visited to see the sick. We were lucky if we got any medicine.

When we really got ill we had to find our way to the nearby town and wait for hours in a long line to see the doctors who worked in the government hospital. These doctors were never in a mood to sing songs to us. Never mind songs, they seldom had the kindness to say something nice to us.

Such times we were worse than dogs.

Bhurus was lucky. He was from the river house. The river house was a rich house. That made all the difference.

Everybody in the river house waited anxiously for the year-end. That was special. My Boss always stopped work at that time and the Boss' children, the Boy and the Girl, came back to the river house for their holidays. Our Madam was the one who got excited most.

'My babies are coming, I can't wait to see them,' she would tell anyone who came within hearing range as the day of arrival came closer.

The Madam certainly got excited when the year was coming to an end. Her babies were coming.

I always went with Madam and Harrison to the airport when her babies came. I was the airport expert. Harrison always took me along whenever he went to the airport. We went often to pick up the Master or to drop him when he went away to drive his aerobblane. That's what he called it, aerobblane. It is the one he took people in and dropped them off at different places. Harrison told me all this, about Master and his aerobblane. Our airport trips were always in the night. I think these aerobblanes never came and went when it was daytime.

We were a good airport team, Harrison and I. He drove the van and I loaded and unloaded the bags. The dropping part was simple. We drove to the airport and as we stopped I ran and got a trolley-bus. By the time the Master got off, I had already finished loading the bags on to the trolley-bus.

The next part was always interesting, pushing this stupid

trolley-bus to the gate. That was again my job. All the airport trolley-buses had wheels that went the way they wanted, in all directions, like madmen in a madhouse. It was very difficult to control. That's what I liked about pushing the trolley-bus. You have to be an expert. I think I was very good at it. I pushed this way and I pushed that way, pulled a little, and twisted a little, and I always got the trolley-bus to go the way I wanted. Even the Master knew I was the best - that's why he always let me push them.

As I said before, the dropping part was easy.

The picking part was a little bit more complicated. Everything depended on me. Harrison knew the dates when they would come. Sometimes it was the Master, sometimes it was the Madam and sometimes it was both the Madam and the Master. Whoever came, our job was the same. Just to go to the airport and do the picking up. It only changed when the Boy and the Girl arrived. Then Madam also joined our airport team and went with us to kiss and bring her babies home.

Now about this picking part; you see the policemen at the airport didn't like if we stopped our van at the gate. They did not allow us to stay there. They blew whistles and chased us. We couldn't wait; we had to go. Harrison had to stop the van outside. There was a special place for vans in a far corner of the airport. All the vans that came to pick up people were parked there.

This is where I became a very important man in our airport team.

Harrison had to wait in the van and I went to the gate to meet the Master or Madam. I was the pickup man; those are my Master's words. The dropping part was never a problem, but the picking part always made me a bit worried.

Lots of people came out from the airport gate at the same time.

Sam's Story

So many were waiting outside. Everyone was standing on their toes and stretching their necks like paddyfield cranes to see who was coming. People pushed and shoved. You know what people are like. They cursed and fought, all trying to squeeze their heads in front to see who was coming.

I didn't have to do all that. I didn't have to be a paddy field crane or push and shove. I always brought my little kitchen bench with me. Just stood on it and I was the tallest. That is experience for you; so many visits to the airport had made me an expert. I knew exactly what to do. The bench and me together were taller than all the cranes that had come to do the picking up.

'You must watch like a hawk.' That's what Harrison told me every time I got off with my little bench to become the pickup man.

So I would stand on my little bench and watch like a hawk, not taking my eyes off the gate even for a second. As soon as I saw Master or Madam I got off my bench and ran to them to tell the team is here, Harrison and I. Then I ran back to the van to bring Harrison. We both came in the van and picked whoever we came to pick up. I loaded the bags and Harrison drove home.

You see, everything in this picking up business depended on me. If not for me the Master and Madam would wait outside the airport without even knowing that Harrison had come. As for Harrison, he would be fast asleep in the van till the sun came up. That's why they needed me, to watch like a hawk and to run like a bat out of hell.

All this bird talk I learnt from the river house, this hawk and bat and things like that. Sometimes I was a hawk and sometimes I was a bat.

It was always funny and I used to laugh whenever I thought of these bird names. To imagine myself with wings and a beak and sitting in some tall tree, watching everything like a hawk, or for that matter, a beakless black Sam Bat rushing out of hell.

One thing good about going to the airport was that I was the only one who could go. Harrison never took Leandro. There was no stupid democracy here and voting with matchsticks when deciding who went to the airport. Leandro had no choice. People like him cannot go to the airport. The soldiers always stopped them. They stopped us too, but they would let us go when we showed our government pictures. Harrison said he didn't like going to the airport with Leandro. His name always made the soldiers suspicious, not the Leandro part, but the rest of it that was very long and very Tamil sounding.

'Too much trouble'. That's what Harrison told me.

Anyway, that holiday too Madam and I went with Harrison to the airport to pick up her babies.

The year-end holidays were long for the Boy and the Girl. They stayed many days. Everything happened in the river house when they were home. These were my enjoyably very busy days. I think I already told you that.

This business of Christmas was very big in the river house. Our river house had different gods. Except for Bhurus and Lena, everybody in the river house had their own gods. Leandro and Janet had their giants and their ones with the six hands and I had mine with the eyes closed. The Master and Madam and the children had their own God nailed to a cross. That river house must have been well protected with all these gods watching and taking good care over it. Come to think of it, that may have been why it was so rich. Many gods must be much better than one God.

We had only one God for our whole village. No wonder the people in my village were all so poor.

It was the Master's daughter, the Girl who told me what this Christmas business was all about.

Sam's Story

'It is his birthday Sam,' she explained. 'Christmas is the day that our Lord was born.' That part she said very seriously, almost as if she was praying.

'The whole world celebrates Christmas, Sam. It is a time for everyone to be happy'.

Now I knew what this Christmas was all about. It is one big birthday party, for everyone to be happy.

All of us at the river house got excited when it came close to the date of Christmas. Madam made special things to eat. It was the three of them who did this special cooking - Madam, Janet and the Girl, but not the stupid Leandro. They made cake, that one I knew. The other food they made I had never seen before. Even the Madam's cake was very different to the cakes I have seen. *Kade Mudalali* used to bring box cakes when our New Year was around. We never bought them. We only saw them. They were very different to what was being made in the river house.

The whole kitchen smelled nice when Madam was making her cake. All the little eating things they made for Christmas looked very sweet and very nice. They baked everything in our oven and then stored them in Leandro's kitchen.

'We will only eat when it is Christmas'. She told us, locking all the sweets in the kitchen cupboard. That was the end of the food part.

But there was so much more for this Christmas business than the things we made to eat.

Janet, Leandro and I became very busy cleaning and polishing everything that was there in the river house. My Madam and her daughter were busy too. They brought boxes of beautiful cards called happy cards and sent them to everyone they knew. Madam wrote cards even to the people who lived down our own road.

Those cards were not posted; I took them and gave them by hand.

Janet, Leandro and me, we were also given cards to send to our homes. Janet and Leandro wrote theirs with their stupid dot and round letters that even my Madam couldn't understand. Their language was as complicated as the two of them. The Girl wrote my card. It was to my mother and my family. The card was a very shining card in red and blue and a lot of gold colour.

My mother would have never got a card like that. The Girl wrote each one's name, my mother's, my sister's and even my brothers. I let her write; I didn't say anything about them not being there.

She wrote my name at the bottom and she said she put loving son. That sounded nice. I'm sure it would have made my mother happy.

We put the card in an envelope and I pasted the stamp myself. I felt very excited.

It was the first time I had sent a happy card.

I didn't know about my mother, but I was very sure my sisters would like my happy card. They always liked things that were beautiful. They didn't get too much of that. So a shining card with all colours and gold lines would be a big thing to them. That's why I felt happy.

As for my brothers, I didn't know what to think.

The Madam and her daughter made lists of things for Christmas. What had to be done and what had to be bought. Harrison often went up and down to the town carrying Madam's lists. Sometimes I went too, whenever he needed someone to load his shopping.

The shops in the town were always full, so were the pavements, with so many people selling so many things. People walked everywhere, from shop to shop. I noticed that most of them went in with nothing and came out also with nothing, just looking at things in the shops and walking away, dragging their children with them.

Harrison said they are the poor people.

'They also want to have Christmas Sam, if they can't have it, at least they come to look at it.'

There certainly were very many people looking at Christmas.

'This Christmas is only for the rich Sam, it is not for people like you and me.'

I don't know why Harrison said that. But he sounded serious. It didn't matter to me whether I had it or not. I didn't even know there was a thing called Christmas till I came to the river house.

As for me, Christmas time was a nice time. The Boy and the Girl were home. The Madam was happy. Master didn't go to work; he just sat and drank his Russians that I made for him. The house looked clean and it smelt like Christmas cake. Even the weather became nice, not hot at all. The winds that came from the river were always cool.

I liked this Christmas time.

It was again the Girl who told me about the man called Santa Claus. She always tried to teach me things I didn't know. She showed me a picture of this fat man in red, wearing big black shoes. He had a smiling face. This man must have been very old. He had very white hair and a very long white beard and he was still going about in a funny cart that had no wheels. The girl said the old man was called Santa Claus.

'Wait and see Sam, he will bring you some nice presents.'

She told me all about this Santa Claus. She said he came once a year, when it was Christmas time. The Girl said that this Santa Claus man always came in the same cart with the same animals pulling it, just to give gifts to everyone on Christmas day. She told me how he would keep the things he brought for us under a special tree that we were going to make for Christmas.

I didn't believe any of that. The Girl sometimes spoke stupid things. We had so many trees in our village and no man ever came in a cart and left gifts for anyone. I didn't want to tell her that, I mean about the stupid part.

We did make a tree for Santa Claus.

This tree we made was a funny tree. Madam had it all packed in a box and she took it out the day before their God's birthday. The boy was the expert. He knew what to do and how to fix the branches. They were all in little plastic pieces and we had to put them together to make the tree. I was the one who helped the boy to get this tree going. Once all the pieces were in place, it became a very tall tree with branches spreading in all directions. Then we hung so many things on it.

First I thought what we hung were our presents. I was rather disappointed. They were just stupid things, good for children. It was the Girl who explained things to me.

'They are not our presents, Sam. These are only for show. Just to make the tree look nice for Santa Claus.' That's what she said.

We really hung some funny things in that Christmas tree. There were shining balls of all colours, red balls, green balls, yellow balls, blue balls, and all kinds of balls. All sizes too, small ones, large ones and large small ones, all shining. These balls were very delicate. If you dropped them, they went to pieces. It was not I; it was Janet who broke a red ball. She dropped and it went to pieces. I had to bring the broom and sweep what was left of that broken red ball.

There were also little golden bells for the tree; they made no noise, silent bells in every branch. They just hung there. We had funny dolls too, pretty dolls called angel dolls with little wings made of white cotton. These angel dolls were all over the tree, hanging by strings that were attached to their heads.

What I liked most in that whole tree thing were the lights. I am a light man; I love lights. That you already know. These lights we had on the tree were really nice lights. Small and in different colours and they went on and off on their own, just like *kalamadiriyo*, fireflies. First I thought the boy was playing tricks on me, slowly going up and down with a switch. It wasn't so, he showed me. The lights came on and went off on their own.

Now we had the tree ready for Santa Claus, the man who came in the cart to give us gifts.

The tree was kept right in the middle of the house. It was beautiful. Lights flashing like fireflies, balls shining in all colours and the gold bells hanging in silence. The little angel dolls with their white cotton wings were always dancing, swinging and spinning from their heads every time the standing fan sent the wind that way.

If what the girl said was true, I was sure that this Santa Claus would be happy with our tree and would leave some nice things for us.

However stupid it sounded I somehow hoped that this Santa Claus man would leave something for me.

I was always the first to get up in the river house. I woke, washed and then started sweeping the garden. That was the normal way I started the day. That morning, before I did anything, I went to check our Christmas tree. I was really surprised, almost shocked would be more correct. The girl was right. There were so many big parcels there; just scattered and lying under the tree. Each one was wrapped in bright coloured paper; so many parcels.

I didn't know which one was mine. I didn't care. There were so many, I was sure there would be one for me too.

Everyone in the river house got up early that morning and they all came charging, straight to the tree, including my Master and my Madam. The Master's daughter was the one who was most excited, she was like a little girl, giggling and laughing and grabbing all the parcels. She took charge of the distribution; she was good at these things. One by one she read the names written on the parcels and one by one she gave each one their gift. The man in the cart had made sure every parcel had a name. I couldn't believe someone would be so nice to leave so many things for us and take the trouble to neatly label them with our names.

Everybody was in a happy mood, laughing and tearing the paper wrappings to see what they got.

Janet, Leandro and me, we got three parcels each. The first one I opened was a shirt, nice shining silver buttons and two pockets. It was a white shirt with little blue and red dots. The dots were very pretty, more like little stars. The shirt was very pretty too. I have never seen such a pretty shirt in my life and I have never seen a shirt with two pockets. My second parcel was a sarong; it had lines in different colours, each going in a different direction. Every colour I knew was there and some that I didn't even know. I loved that sarong. The third gift I got was a small parcel, very small. As I opened it, I felt so happy, that I laughed like a fool.

It was a belt, just what I always wanted, to tie around my waist, a brown belt with a gold buckle. I always wanted to get a nice belt. I had one, a white one that someone had given my sister Loku. But it was very old and torn; some of the holes had joined each other. This new brown belt was a real gift. That Santa Claus man must have been very clever to leave me with the exact thing I wanted.

Sam's Story

In all my life I cannot remember a single day anyone had given me anything. It's true that I don't remember much. But some things I remember well. I knew for sure that no one had ever given me a present. This gift and present business was something very new to me. I learnt these things only after I came to the river house.

So here I was, on my Master's God's birthday, not one, but with three gifts in my hand. I just didn't know what to say. The old man in the cart had gone off in the night itself. I didn't even know him, only knew his name and what he looked like. I thought this Santa Claus must have been a very nice man to leave me with all these beautiful presents.

When things became quiet, after the excitement of presents, I spoke to the Girl. I was a bit confused, with this God's birthday business and the tree and the Santa Claus man leaving nice things for us. I asked her whether it was possible for people to change their God.

'Why Sam? Why would anyone want to change their God?'

Then I told her.

I think she got upset. She stayed silent, looking at me in a funny way. I didn't want to upset her. I told her I asked only because no one in our house had ever got any present. I was sure Loku and Podi wouldn't mind changing gods and making a tree for the Santa Claus man. Especially if they also got belts, dresses and bags like Janet did. I told her that.

'No Sam, I don't think it is a good idea,' her voice went soft and got almost lost. I think I saw traces of tears in her eyes as she got up and ran upstairs.

I never spoke again about the cart man or about changing gods. Somehow, the thrill I had of getting presents was not all that thrilling anymore. It must have had something to do with what I thought of home.

Lot of people came to the river house during Christmas time. We were all very busy. Leandro cooked from morning till night. Janet was also sent to the kitchen to help when there was too much cooking to be done. I was very busy too. Opening and closing the gate alone took a lot of doing. So many cars came, so many cars went. Every car had so many people; all coming to visit the river house for Christmas. They all ate my Madam's food and drank from my Boss' bar.

So who do you think made all the drinks?

It was me all the time. I had never been so busy in my life, so many cars, so many visitors and so many drinks to make. Sometimes when there were too many people the Girl also helped me to make the drinks. She was nice, I liked her, but she was not like the Boy. She and I had little in common. Only making drinks when there were too many people. But she was always kind, she always tried to teach and explain things to me.

This Christmas time at the river house lasted till the year changed. Every evening there were visitors. Many of them stayed for dinner. There was so much food in the house; a lot of it went to waste. The iceboxes in Leandro's kitchen were full and overflowing all the time.

Most of the people who came to the river house for Christmas were known to me. There was a lot of laughing, shouting, hugging and Christmas wishing when people arrived. The visitors came with gifts and got gifts. 'What a beautiful present' and 'Why did you' and 'so nice' and 'our pleasure' and 'You didn't have to spend so much' - that kind of talk went like ping pong balls, back and forth, from one to another. The gifts were always viewed and admired even before the visitors had a chance to sit.

Everyone brought gifts for the family. Some of them, I mean

Sam's Story

the regulars, brought gifts for Janet too. As for Leandro and me, they didn't give gifts; they gave money.

I don't know why nobody gave gifts to Leandro and me.

'Sam, happy Christmas,' they always said that part. The rest was different. Like thieves, they quietly passed money into our hands. The most we got was a 'Keep this'. No fuss, just money, passed from hand-to-hand like pickpockets.

My Master's brother was the best; he gave me money twice. Must have forgotten the first time. Even Velu's Madam gave me money. She was always nice; she was the one who always petted Bhurus and Lena whenever she came to the river house. 'Happy Christmas, Sam' she said to me whilst giving me the money. She said that to Bhurus and Lena too and laughed loud. Lena ignored her, but Bhurus, being stupid, barked.

Most evenings when we had visitors, the Boy sent fire-sticks over the river. He called them skyrockets. I was the one who bravely stood with him and passed him his rockets. Everyone in the house came to the garden to watch the Boy and me send skyrockets.

They were like flying snakes, these rockets.

Ssssshooooosh, ...bang, that's how they went.

They sped into the dark night spilling fire and then exploded with a loud noise, spreading beautiful flower-like fire drops all over the sky. The Boy was the expert and I was his assistant.

'We make a good team Sam,' the Boy always said, patting my head, after the fireworks were over.

I must have been a good team man. Everybody wanted to team with me; like Harrison, when he went to the shops and the airport and the Girl when we poured drinks for the visitors. Even my Master spoke about the good team when we threw green balls to feed the fish in the pond.

Sam, the team man; I am sure they all must have felt good to be in my team.

That's how my Christmas went about. It was a good time. I wore my striped sarong and tied my gold buckled belt. With that I wore my white shirt with red and blue little stars. Everyone who came to the river house said I looked good. I ate my Madam's cake, as much as I wanted and ate all the other things that tasted so sweet, again, as much as I wanted. The days just rolled and ran like a fast train.

This Christmas time in the river house was a very good time indeed, the best I can ever remember.

The Girl was the one who told me about the important visitor who was coming to the river house. She was our Boy's friend, our Boy's special friend. She was someone who was learning with them in that far away school. She was coming to spend some time at the river house; this special friend would stay with us. That's what the Girl told me.

'She's my friend too Sam, she is very nice and she is very pretty. You'll like her.'

I think I already liked her. The Boy was my good friend and the visitor was our Boy's special friend. So how not to like her?

The special visitor came to the river house a few days after the year changed. She was on holiday in Sri Lanka and the Girl and the Boy had invited her to stay with us.

I think her family lived in some other country and her father was a doctor. That is what I gathered from what I heard.

It was the Boy who went with his sister to pick up the special friend. We were all looking forward to meeting her. Even the Master and Madam were waiting for the special friend to come. They had met her before, when they visited the children in their far away school.

Sam's Story

I still remember how I waited by the river house gate, waiting for the car to come with our Boy's special friend. I even practised my special smile a few times, just to make sure that I would get it right and give her my best.

As it turned out, all that was in vain. I hated her even before she came to our doorstep.

I was the first one who greeted the special friend when the Boy and the Girl drove her home. She got out of the car with a broad smile saying 'Hello Hello Sammy,' and added something more in English, which I didn't understand. I kept giving her my special welcome grin. All that was fine.

Then she turned to Leandro and spoke to him in their own language.

Leandro and Janet were bad enough. That stupid Velu's visits to the river house made it worse. I didn't need any more additions of their kind. Boy or no Boy, special friend or no special friend, from that first word she spoke to Leandro I knew from where she was and I hated her.

This visitor turned out to be one very big problem to me. She certainly became the biggest disappointment I had in my Master's river house.

I never came inside the house when this special friend was around. I minded my own business and spent my time with Bhurus and Lena in the garden. Sometimes that was also not possible. The Boy would come with her and sit by the river. The Boy would talk to me and she also tried to talk and become friends. Such times I ran inside the house and pretended to do some other work. I always had to hide from her.

I didn't want to become her friend. In any case she couldn't speak to me. She only knew her language and English and she didn't know mine. The most she did was say 'Hello Sam, Hello Sam,' and grin at me. In a way that was good, no language, no talk. I didn't want to talk to her.

I felt sorry for our Boy. He was my good friend. He is a nice boy. I didn't know why he had to have special friends with people who threw bombs and killed our soldiers.

I think the Master's daughter knew that I didn't like this new visitor. She knew I hated their kind. Maybe that is why she tried to explain things to me several times.

She told me that everybody who belonged to that kind didn't throw bombs to kill soldiers.

'They are just like us Sam, most of them are very nice people.'

I silently listened.

'There is nothing wrong with Leandro and Janet and our friend here Sam,' she went on to defend them. 'These people don't throw bombs; they don't kill anybody. They are just like us.'

I never said anything to her. I only listened.

During that time, when the Boy's special friend stayed in the river house, the Girl often spoke to me about this matter of me hating the other kind.

'It is wrong to hate people who we don't even know Sam,' she tried to convince me.

I don't think she knew many things. She hardly knew anything that happened in our country. She stayed far away in her school and came to the river house only for the holidays to fold napkins on the dinner table and pour wine and twist her wine bottles.

She's been gone too long. Maybe that is why she spoke like that.

There were times that I wanted to tell her that it was not I, but it was she who was wrong.

But I just didn't know how.

I don't think people can tell other people what they really feel, about who is right and who is wrong. It is difficult; especially when some things are buried deep inside and are too sad to talk about.

That's why I never told her. That's why I only listened.

My War

The elections were over, so were the promises. There was a lot of disappointment in our village after they selected the leaders. People had kept high hopes and thought things would change. Nothing changed. We remained the same, dirt poor, discarded and hopeless.

But for a few others things did change.

Kaluwa's father, *Kade Mudalali*, became a big man overnight. His colour had won, so he became the biggest man in the area. Everybody had to go to him for everything. People who were close to him also became small big men. Not as big as *Kade Mudalali*, but big enough for all of us to know they were big.

When the factory was built *Kade Mudalali* became the most important man. The factory was going to make shirts, to send to far away lands for white men to wear. They needed girls to work in the garment factory. Those who got jobs to make shirts were all selected and sent by *Kade Mudalali*.

He was now the big boss in our village. People even said that he got money for just sending people to the factory. Kaluwa too went to work there. He was also a boss in the factory, that's what he told us. He had only to walk around and look at the girls and make sure they stitched the buttons right. He got paid for doing that. Some job. He said other things too, about the girls and what he did with them when the factory work was over. I didn't believe him. He was always a liar, just like his father.

Sam's Story

Our village got a mail place after the elections. It was *Kade Mudalali* who arranged it through his friends in our new government. He decided that the best place to have the mail office was his own shop and the best one to work there was his own daughter, Ossiya. So that's where they made the new mail place. In a little room they built next to *Kade Mudalali's* shop. They called it a sub mail office. It was a small mail office.

The nearest mail place was in town and that was miles away. The sub mail office was not only for our village but also for the mail that came to the whole area.

Ossiya left school and became the mail woman. She sat behind a small window and sold stamps and things like that. When the mail came, she was the one who sorted it out and kept it for people to come and collect. There was not much mail. People in villages didn't get many letters. That meant Ossiya did not have much work to do. But she got paid. It was Kaluwa's father's government which paid her. Just to sit behind the window and sell stamps.

The biggest thing that happened in our village after the elections was when they fixed a telephone into the sub mail office. I think it was not for any of us but mainly for Kaluwa's father to talk to his friends in the big city. Though the telephone was in the mail office, everyone knew it was *Kade Mudalali's* phone, paid by his government for the things he had done for them before the elections. Having a telephone and getting telephone calls made *Kade Mudalali* even bigger than he already was.

Everybody came to look at the sub mail office telephone. People in my village had no idea about telephones. They never knew anyone who had them. They had no calls to make nor anybody to call them. But still they came to see. If they were lucky, the telephone would ring and Kaluwa's sister Ossiya would say

'Hallo Hallo.' Other than *Kade Mudalali*, she was the only one who knew how to do the 'HalloHallo'. Ossiya and *Kade Mudalali* were also the only ones who knew how to roll numbers in the telephone and make calls to the city.

The sub mail office and the telephone were the only things our village got from the elections. They were both useless to us. Of course the factory was there. But it gave jobs only to Kaluwa's father's people.

Again, useless.

Things became very difficult for my mother at that time. She was often sick, too sick to go out and tap rubber. A lot of times she stayed home and slept, curled on her mat.

Sometimes she coughed so much and got so weak that we got scared and took her to the hospital in town. We did it many times. Each time it was the same. She got sick, we got scared and we somehow managed to get her to the hospital in town.

It was by borrowing money from Kaluwa's father that we found the bus fare. We had to plead, almost beg to get a few rupees. Loku was the one who always went to meet *Kade Mudalali*.

Going to town with a sick person was not easy. First we had to walk about two miles to the road and then we had to wait a long time for the bus. We had done it a few times so we knew exactly what to do. Loku is the one who wrapped our mother's head in a towel and made her warm and Jaya carried her. That's how we went. She was too weak to walk. Loku and I always went along; Loku to talk to the doctors and me because I was the eldest.

We didn't have enough money for the bus. Otherwise we would have taken Podi and Madiya too, just for support.

At the hospital we had to take numbers and wait in a long line to meet the doctor. It was always the same every time we went.

Sam's Story

After all the waiting, maybe hours, the doctor only saw my mother for a few minutes. He made her cough and wrote something in a paper and gave us. That was the medicine she had to take.

'Must get your mother to eat well, good food to make her strong,' the doctor would always say to my sister. Loku would nod too, it was her "no problem" nod, as if we had an icebox full of food at home to feed and make our mother strong.

Most of the medicines my mother had to take were not available in the hospital. It would have been easy if they had them. The government hospital medicine was free for poor people like us. But most times the man in the hospital store made a sour face and shook his head.

'We don't have this anymore, maybe next week the stocks will come.'

We knew the answer by heart. That is what he always said whenever we went to the hospital and tried to get medicine from him.

'You can buy it from the pharmacy,' Sour face always gave the same advice.

We never bought any pharmacy medicine. We barely had enough money for the bus to get back home.

We had no icebox full of food either to keep our mother well fed.

The only thing that happened by going to the hospital was we owed more money to *Kade Mudalali*.

But we still went when my mother got sick. That is all we knew to do. Just go and see the doctor and get the medicine paper and hear the hospital store man tell us when the next stock was coming.

My mother's sicknesses came and went. She became better not by any hospital visit or by any doctor's medicine but maybe by sheer luck. I think this was one time the gods looked slowly to our side, maybe a glance or two. However sick she became somehow she always got better.

Even though we were poor, the gods owed us something too, at least for all the praying my mother did and all the *kankun* and *gotukola* we ate in their name.

I think that was how my mother survived.

After the river over-flowed our house was not a house anymore, just a roof and some planks and a few coconut leaves that were covering the sides. The river had reduced it to that. Things were getting really bad. I think everybody in our house expected my sister to get a job in the garment factory. That's what they promised before the elections.

'It would have been nice if Loku got the job,' my mother said it a thousand times and it was always with a sigh.

'There would have been money in the house to buy food and money to do other things.' That also she said a thousand times and finished with the same sigh.

There was never a job, no money, almost nothing to eat, let alone money to do other things.

My days too went from nothing to nothing. My friend Piya was no more. I missed him. He and I used to spend a lot of time together. Now he was gone. I had nobody to be with. I never drove cars by myself. There was no fun in it without Piya. We used to hear Piya's mother cry almost every night. It took a long time for her to stop crying. It took a longer time for me to stop thinking of Piya. I tried to remember some of the things he said. But I forgot. I only remembered how we drove our cars and how we sat by the river and watched people bring the sand up.

It was this time that I got a job to work at Madam Martell's as a houseboy. The same time my two brothers went to join the army, to kill the people who were trying to divide our country.

Sam's Story

I came to Colombo to my new home and new job. It was Piya's uncle, *Podi Maama,* who brought me. He worked as a night watchman at Madam Martell's. I was very lucky. Piya's watcher uncle came visiting to our village, to see his sister. He stayed a few days at Piya's house. I think it was Piya's mother who told him to get me a job. One day he came to our house and asked me whether I would like to go to Colombo with him, to work in his master's big house. He said his master was a white man, not short and flat faced like the factory white men. Normal face, a tall man.

'Good job, good pay, you can eat as much as you want,' he said in a boastful manner touching his big stomach which spilled out of his tight wide belt.

'He will come with you; he is a good boy. He can do anything,' my mother had jumped and answered before I could even think.

It was settled then and there. We all walked to *Kade Mudalali's* shop to take a telephone call. Piya's *Podi Maama* was very keen to take me. He knew I could do anything. He even paid for the call. He went inside and spoke to someone on the telephone. We waited outside, my mother and I.

A while later he came out and told us everything was arranged. He had spoken to his madam and she had said to bring me. I'm sure he must have told her that I could do anything.

Podi Maama's madam would have felt very lucky to have me coming to work in her house.

That is how I got my first job. I was going to be a *boyi kolla* in Colombo in a white madam's house.

My mother and I walked back home after the telephone call. I had never seen my mother in a mood like that. I think she was very happy. She couldn't stop smiling. Even her walk was different, light and fast. I noticed the way she went past the little mud puddles on our gravel path. She didn't go round them; she leapt over them like a little girl. She sure looked very excited and was in a hurry to reach home.

It was one of the few times I remember that we were all really happy and there was the sound of laughter in our one roomed house.

The next day I left the village.

I had nothing much to take, so each one in my family gave me something of their own. Loku, my big sister, gave me her white belt and Podi gave me her comb. My brothers, Jaya the elder one gave a *baniyama* and Madiya the little one, a new sarong he had preserved and kept. My mother had nothing to give. So she touched my head and pleaded with her gods to bless me and take care of me.

I knelt and kissed her feet and hugged the rest of them and said good-bye. There were tears in everyone's eyes. It is true we were poor and we never had much, but we've always had each other. The six of us had been together in that one roomed shack and had done our best to make something of our lives. Now I was leaving and even for poor people like us that was sad.

It was all written on my mother's face. I saw it as I turned and walked away.

Everything I had to take with me was in a brown paper bag. The new sarong, old *baniyama*, white belt and Podi's comb all packed and folded. That's how I left home on my way to my new job in Colombo. My family stood outside our house and watched me go; my mother still crying, the others waving their hands in a silent good-bye. They watched me walk away with a pretended light step, jumping over the little mud puddles in the path.

Sam's Story

It was the same month that the military men came to our area. They visited villages to get young boys to join the military to become soldiers. They needed more men to go and fight in the war. The military men wanted everybody. Anyone over school age was invited to join. That's how both Jaya and Madiya went to become soldiers, to be heroes in the army and to stop people from dividing our country.

From the first day itself I didn't like very much working in Madam Martell's house. The people there were not nice. Madam Martell's husband was also white. He was a very tall thin man who played cards with his white friends. He was always playing cards at home or going out to play cards, a real card man. That's all he did.

The card man never spoke to me. I don't think that he even spoke one word to me for all the time I worked in his house. He just looked at me and looked the other way, as if I was never there. Madam Martell also had very little to do with me.

'What's his name?' That's what she first asked when I arrived in her house with Piya's *Podi Maama*.

He translated. I told her my name.

'Too long, too long, too long' she shook her head from side to side and repeated like a talking parrot.

'You'll be Sam.'

She never asked me whether I liked the name or not. That was it. No questions. She just decided what I should be called. Old name gone, new name Sam.

Now you know how I came to be called Sam.

All because that stupid white madam thought that my name was too long.

It was the cook woman, Sopi Akka, who was my boss in that

Colombo house. She was the one who ordered me around. She was a fat woman, well fed, having been in the Martell home for a long time. Her body was very big and she had a huge backside, the buttocks were like two bullock cartwheels joined together. They rolled and rocked when Sopi Akka walked. Her breasts too were big, like inflated balloons. Often I have seen Sopi Akka's breasts jutting out of the bottom of her loose jacket like peeping quarter moons. All this was because she was old and fattened and well fed by Martell food. I think Sopi Akka was quite old even though she liked doing things that young women did.

Sopi Akka wasn't all that bad, just moody and pure lazy and a little bit more complicated than all that.

'*Kolla* bring me this, and *Kolla* bring me that.' That's what she always said whenever she saw me.

'*Kolla* do this, do that, or *Kolla* wash this and wipe that.' She never failed to order me to do something.

I was also new to this '*boyi kolla*' job and didn't know what exactly I had to do. So I did everything Sopi Akka ordered. I didn't mind the work in Madam Martell's house. There was nothing much to do, but there was nobody to talk to. That was the difficult part. Piya's *Podi Maama* only came in the night to be the watcher and he left early in the morning, sometimes even before I got up. There was only Sopi Akka the cook, Madam Martell, her husband and me the houseboy, who lived there.

So who to talk to?

That's why I wasn't happy there. I always felt very lonely at Madam Martell's house.

Podi Maama told me that every month I would get a pay and he would collect it from Madam Martell and send it to my mother.

'That is the arrangement, your mother agreed,' he explained.

That was fine with me. I didn't need any money. I knew it

would make my mother happy to get some money. She could eat with it and do other things, as she always wanted to do. Since my brothers went to become soldiers there was only Loku, Podi and my mother and our chickens. They could all eat well with my money.

Life at Madam Martell's house was really nothing. I just went from day to day doing my daily chores with no one to talk to.

Sometimes Sopi Akka would speak to me. It was mainly to complain. She always complained about everything. If the sun was shining, she complained it was too hot. When it rained she protested there was no sun. If we ate rice, she complained it was not bread. If we ate bread, she grumbled it was not hoppers. When we drank tea, she preferred coffee, and when it was coffee, she wanted to drink tea. She had some complaint for everything that happened in that house. She complained about her family too. She told me about her son who was married.

'She is a prime bitch Sam, a real *moosali*,' she used bad words like that when she described her son's wife. 'My son was finished from the day he married that whore.' Sopi Akka really had choice words of description when it came to that woman.

'Never allowed my son to give me anything, not a cent. Let alone that, never allowed him to even come and see me.'

I realised that Sopi Akka's number one enemy in life was her son's wife, the *moosali*. She sometimes complained about her husband too, who was already dead.

'Useless fellow, drank all the time.'

The drunkard husband got off mildly compared to the daughter-in-law. If Sopi Akka ever spoke to me, it was always something unpleasant about something that was wrong. I guess I was the only one around in that house that she could complain to. Madam Martell didn't care. In any case she did not understand our language; it was useless telling her anything.

I never could figure out why Sopi Akka brought out all her sad stories to me, as if I could change things for her. Maybe she did so thinking I had some answers for her. She didn't realise it was useless. I couldn't stop the days from being hot, I couldn't bring back her husband from the dead and take his drinking out and I sure didn't know what to do about her son's whore. I guess people just complain, even when they know very well there are no answers to their complaints.

Maybe she did so for me to feel sorry for her. That is what she said one night when she came to my mat and sat next to me.

'There's no one for me Sam; I am all alone and lonely. Don't you feel sorry for me?'

I couldn't figure that one.

It's only when she began to send her hands all over me that I realised what was happening. She started with my face and then went to my neck and to my chest and to my body. All the time she was whispering and sweet-talking me through her semi-toothed mouth saying there was no one for her in this world. She carried on the search, groping in the dark like a blind woman, going further down, past my stomach to where my things were.

It was the first time someone had touched my things.

I was a bit scared, but I felt fine. I felt excited. Her huge body was leaning heavily on me and her large breasts had flattened and spread all over my face and chest. I didn't know what to do. So I stayed still and moaned till it all happened.

That was all.

She left as silently as she came.

She never spoke in the morning about her visit to my mat and all that took place in the night. She only gave me more to eat and even fried me an egg.

Sopi Akka did repeat her visits from time to time; not very often, but once in a while. I didn't care, I did nothing, she did everything and I felt fine. I bet she felt fine too, that is why she kept coming back to my mat in the night to flatten her breasts on my face and to tell me how lonely she was. It was always followed by her slow search for my things.

There was as usual the reward of a fried egg in the morning.

Once Sopi Akka asked about my family and my home. I lied. I told her that my father had a shop and we had a telephone. I told her my sister worked in the mail office and my brother worked in a factory. I told her Kaluwa's story as if it was mine. It was a good story. I didn't want to tell about our half house and our chicken and about my mother tapping rubber.

'Then you must be very rich,' she said that and laughed loud. I think she was happy that I came from a rich family. I also kept pretending that I was rich.

Other than these occasional small talk, we mostly kept to ourselves. Sopi Akka was happy that she had someone to order around and I was happy there was someone to tell me how to get about my work as a houseboy. Madam Martell's husband ignored us and played cards and Madam Martell hardly spoke to us.

The days simply came and went with nothing in between.

With time, I learnt a few things at Madam Martell's house. The best was the telephone. When Sopi Akka and I were alone, she always told me to answer the telephone. She was too lazy to get up and roll her bullock cartwheel arse to answer the bell. I knew how to do it. I have seen how Kaluwa's sister took it and said 'hallo hallo'. The first time I tried answering the phone I think I made a mess of it. I didn't know which side spoke and which side listened. I kept saying 'hallo hallo' and heard nothing. It took me awhile to sort this out. But after that I became an expert at answering the telephone.

Of course I never spoke to the people who called. They never spoke my language. Sopi Akka is the one who taught me what to say.

'Hallo hallo, not at home,' that's all I had to say. Madam Martell and her husband were not at home. That is why I answered the telephone.

One day I was in the garden when Madam Martell shouted at me and gestured with her hand frantically for me to come inside the house. She was very excited and when she got excited she always spoke in her language. She was shouting some words and waving her hand. I ran to the house and she pointed at the telephone.

'For you, for you,' she excitedly repeated.

It was the most pleasant thing that happened to me in Madam Martell's house. The call was for me. It was my mother. Piya's *Podi Maama* had gone visiting his sister and had told my mother she could speak to me on the telephone. My mother was calling from *Kade Mudalali's* mail office. I could hardly hear her, but I knew it was her. She was the only one who spoke to me like that. She was the only one who loved me so much in this world to call me her *"rath-tharan"*.

We said some stupid things to each other. It was happy talk, but we didn't know what to say. We were both talking at the same time. She told me she got my money and she was well and Podi and Loku were also well. I told her what I ate and how big the house and garden were. I asked about our chickens and she said they were also well, laying a lot of big eggs. She said that my brothers Jaya and Madiya had also sent some money to her.

"They are doing very well in the military. They get free food and a lot of money,' she said with some newfound pride.

I asked about her cough and she laughed loud making noises with her throat.

"See, no cough, I eat well now.' She sounded real happy.
She told me why she really called.

'I wanted to hear your voice *Puthey.*' On that she went a bit soft and tender.

'Sometimes I miss you too much *Mage Rath-tharan Puthey,*' she added that part in a mellower tone, almost in a whisper.

I didn't know what to say.

She talked some more and laughed some more. She sure sounded happy. I think it was the best talk I have had with my mother in all my life.

I felt very nice for days just thinking about how she called and the things we spoke about.

Month after month went by and it almost came to the end of the year. I even began to get used to the loneliness at Madam Martell's house. There were always a few problems, but I didn't take any notice. I learnt to ignore. Life was better that way.

Off and on I had to hear Sopi Akka's complaints. They were always the same. After a while I knew them by heart, all except the new versions of her *"moosali"* stories. Sopi Akka's daughter-in-law seemed to be always inventing new ways to make the old woman unhappy.

Once in a way Madam Martell shouted at me in her own language. I didn't understand most of the things she said. The shouting was always for stupid things that she thought were important.

'Don't worry about her,' Sopi Akka took my side when we were back in the kitchen alone. 'The problem with her is that sometimes she thinks the sun shines from her arsehole.'

It didn't bother me none. I didn't care where this white woman fixed the sun. Whether it was in her arsehole or in front.

So I didn't mind.

These were a few of the problems I faced from time to time. A little bit of loneliness, a bit of Sopi Akka's complaints about her family and the weather, then her night visits and the fried egg business and of course where and how Madam Martell fixed the sun under her dress, things like that.

These were just very small problems, if you can call them that.

It was Madam Martell who gave me the telephone message. She said someone called from the village and wanted me to come home that day itself.

'Why?' I asked.

'I don't know,' she said and looked in a funny way at Sopi Akka.

She gave me some money and I left that afternoon. I knew it would be night by the time I reached home. I sat in the bus and watched the road speeding by. I wasn't watching, I was thinking. I didn't know why I was going home. But I didn't feel well.

Somehow I knew that there was something very very wrong at home.

The soldiers came to bury my brother Jaya. They were his friends. The military paid for everything, including the pyre and the firewood. They paid for the chairs that were hired and they paid for the alms that were given to the temple. They paid for everything.

I guess the military men were trying to even the score. Our Jaya had paid them with his life.

The day before the funeral some men from the military came with flags to hang around our house and a big banner with words praising my brother. They also brought hundreds of handbills, small square ones with Jaya's picture in it. He looked nice with the military clothes and his funny hat that went sideways. There were some words in these papers saying that he was a hero.

Sam's Story

The boys in the village helped the military men to paste these papers all over our area. My brother was everywhere, on every house that had a wall, every lamp post on the big road and even in every coconut tree trunk that was anywhere near any place people walked. The military men told my mother that it was for people to know that my brother had died fighting for his country.

Lot of people came to Jaya's funeral; people from the village, people from the town and people from the military. Some big man from the military stood up on a chair and gave a long loud speech. He said my brother was a brave young man. He said words like that praising Jaya. He praised my mother too, for giving her son to the nation. He said nice things about my sisters and me and also about Madiya, my other brother who was still fighting the war.

When he finished, *Kade Mudalali* got up and gave a speech. He also praised my brother and us. Said our family was a great family who produced heroes who fought for the country. One hero was dead, the other hero was still fighting; he said that and repeated it for everybody to hear. I thought he will mention me too, but I guess you can't call a *boyi kolla* who works for a white woman a hero. I think that's why he left me out.

We watched the pyre burn and the flames reach the sky. Then we all came home. The military men had arranged biscuits and bottled drinks to be served after the funeral. People sat on the hired chairs and ate and drank and spoke about Jaya and the war. Someone told me Jaya was shot one night when he was a guard.

My brother had died guarding some unknown road that went to some unheard place.

That night, after the people had left, I sat on my mango tree and kept looking at my world. There had never been much in it, which I always knew and didn't mind. But now even the little there was had changed and had become unbearably sad.

Inside our house I could still hear my mother crying and Loku and Podi saying those meaningless words to console. Our Jaya was dead. Somebody killed him for trying to stop them from dividing the country. If not for this war my brother would still be alive. He would still be unloading vegetable boxes at the town market, or bringing sand from the river, maybe tapping rubber.

Jaya would be here.

Now he was a hero, pasted on a coconut tree trunk with his silly clothes and the funny hat that went sideways. And he was dead.

The military gave some money to my mother. They gave her a picture of my brother too, in a gold coloured frame. He was smiling. It was a good picture. He looked nice. We fixed a nail and hung that picture on our doorpost. Every evening, when the sun went down, my mother lit a lamp under Jaya's picture. She prayed for him every night and most times her praying was mixed with her crying.

My mother didn't want me to go back to Madam Martell's house. She wanted me to stay. She said we could manage. I didn't want to go back either. I didn't want to face the loneliness in the big house. I didn't want to hear Sopi Akka's constant complaints. I didn't want her nighttime visits to my mat and her funny games with my things or to eat her consolation fried eggs in the morning.

So I stayed.

It was almost a month later that my other brother Madiya, the little one, came home. He came in the night, like a thief. He looked tired and haggard. He told us not to tell anybody that he was home.

'The war is over for me.' That's what he told us.

'I will never go back. They will have to kill me before they can take me back again to fight for them.' Madiya sounded very angry when he told us these things.

The first day he slept all the time. He woke up once and ate something and slept again. He slept as if he was dead. We all kept quiet and let him sleep. It was only the second day he woke properly. That too he never went out of the house, mostly lay in his mat and ate everything my mother gave him.

We spoke long that night. I mean he spoke and we listened, my mother, my two sisters and I. He started telling us about the war and what happened in the military. All that was too confusing for me. I always thought the military was a wonderful place. I saw the military men who came to our village when they buried Jaya. They were all nice men. They gave my brother a big funeral. They were kind to my mother and gave her money and said all those nice things about our family when they burned the pyre.

'Don't talk stupid,' my little brother angrily retorted when I mentioned that. 'They are nice when you die,' he spat his words out. 'They are the nicest people when they come to bury you.'

'That war is very different to what you hear about it or what they write in the newspapers. Believe me, I have seen it. They call us cowards and hunt us down like animals when we run away. At least we are the poor bastards who went to fight and we ran when we couldn't take it anymore,' he tried to explain.

'What about those rich people in the big towns?' Madiya asked in a voice that was filled with hatred.

'What about their sons? They never go to fight. It is their country too.' He paused and shook his head.

'No doubt it is their country,' he said in a whisper, his face worn and weary and matching equally the disgust in his voice. 'It is their country, their soldiers, but it is not their war.'

I couldn't figure out most of what he was saying. But I saw the way my mother, Loku and Podi were grasping every word that spilled out of Madiya's mouth. I saw the tears too. I don't know why they cried, but I was pretty sure it must have been for the things I didn't understand.

'These are the people who call us cowards. They call us deserters,' Madiya went on, spilling his anger against the rich people living in towns.

'Where are they? They are not in the camps or on the lonely roads where the killing is going on. They are playing cricket or watching cricket or going to big hotels to eat their meals. They never go to fight. So they don't have to die or run like I did. They don't have to be called cowards. That is the war for you.'

The four of us sat around him in the mat and continued to listen in silence as he went on to tell us about his war.

He said he was in a small camp with about one hundred soldiers. There was a big camp nearby with about two thousand soldiers and there were about twenty-five small camps like his one surrounding the big camp. All the small camps had about a hundred soldiers. He said they called them satellite camps.

'We guarded the main road that connected the camps,' he explained to us. 'Six hours in a bunker watching the road and four hours off and then another six hours in a bunker and another four hours off. That went on non-stop for four months,' he told us what it was like.

'The four hours off was not to sleep. We still had to work in the camp. We had to clean our guns, cut the grass and replace sand bags, so many things. If we were lucky we slept four hours in the night. All this time we waited for the enemy to come, to kill them or for them to kill us.'

He went on and on telling the four of us about the fighting that was going on.

'After four months we were given ten days to go anywhere. Most of the soldiers went and never came back. They are supposed to be the bad ones, the cowards.'

His voice trailed to a softer tone, almost to a whisper and he added 'I am also one of them.'

We didn't know what to say. He sounded so bitter. We didn't know much about this war and who fought whom and for what reasons. We only knew that the boys in the village went to the military and got good pay. That was possibly the only steady job available to people like my two brothers unless they too settled to dig sand from the river or tap rubber.

I always thought the military was a good place to go to work. You became a soldier and you were given a gun and then you killed the enemy and got paid for it.

'What about the other side?' It was Loku my older sister who asked. She knew some things about the war. She wasn't like me. She read newspapers and spoke with her friends about what was happening in the world.

'The other side,' Madiya grinned. 'The other side,' he repeated swinging his head from side to side. 'I think they are worse off than us. Most of them are just children; maybe twelve or ten, maybe younger. A lot of them are young girls. I have seen some of them when their bodies were brought to our camp. Dead with their eyes open. I don't think they know anything more about this war than we do. We kill them because they come to kill us, neither of us knowing why we are doing that to each other.'

He swore again that he didn't want any part in this horrible war and told us he will never go back.

'What's the point? He asked us, as if we knew what the answers were.

'We are fighting and dying and the people in power who want us to fight are sending their children to other countries to keep them away from the war.'

He took a little time off to be silent. We too kept our mouths shut.

'When you join the military you are finished,' he came charging back at us.

'Either you die or you run away and get called a coward. That is how it all ends,' he said that and stopped.

'No, there's another way, a third way too,' he slowly nodded his head as if he just found an additional solution.

'That is if you manage to survive the five years. That's how long you have to be in the military before they let you go. You come out thinking you are a hero. You fought and saved the country from being divided. You think they are all waiting to embrace you and take good care of you.'

There was a grin on his face; it was a sad grin, the likes I have seen when people have only the gods to complain to.

'There are no jobs. Nobody embraces you and no one has employment for men who have sat through nights guarding roads to kill the enemy. No one cares. That is the reality. That is what is really sad. Some of my friends who left after five years came back to the army. They had families to feed. They came back to the same hell so that their children could eat. No one gave them jobs, no one cared.'

Our Madiya said so many things like that. The night got long as he went on and on. It was all to do with this fighting and how terrible the war in the north was. We listened silently, the others wiping their tears from time to time and me doing my best to put pieces together and figure out what he was saying. Occasionally Loku would ask some question. She was the only one who knew something in our house. Madiya spat out his angry answers and continued on.

Sam's Story

I felt that he wasn't just telling these stories for us to know what it was like in the military and what the fighting was all about. It was more like a protest he was making for the absurdity of it all. Since there was no one to protest to, he was left with people like Loku, Podi and my old mother and me to listen to his sad story.

Even though I didn't understand most things he said, I figured out that his story was sad, more like meaningless. That would be the correct word.

Meaningless would be more closer to the truth of what happened in this stupid war.

Madiya left a week later. He never told us where he was going. He only kept repeating that we should never talk about him and never tell anybody that he came home.

'One day, when this miserable war is over, I'll come back.' That's what he said when he stole out that night.

He went the same way he came, like a thief.

Some weeks later the military men came to our house. Four men came in their jeep. One was a big man in the military; the others were just ordinary small military men. This time they were not nice at all. They even shouted at us. They shouted at my mother, then at me and even shouted at my two sisters. They wanted to know where my little brother was.

'We don't know,' that's what we said; just the way Madiya wanted us to tell. They asked again and again and we said again and again that we didn't know.

The big military man said some bad things about Madiya. He said that my brother was not a man; he was a shameless coward who had run away like a frightened chicken. He also said they will put him in jail when they catch him. The military men said they would put us also in jail if we hide him. They said some more bad things, some dirty things too and went away saying they will be back.

The military men never came back to look for him again. My little brother didn't come back either.

It's been so long now.

That is how I lost my two brothers Jaya and Madiya. They went to the military to fight the war, to stop people from dividing our country. The big one became a hero and was buried. The little one became a coward and went missing. We lost them both.

That is why I hated that kind. They can be cooks like the stupid Leandro or slimy bastards like that bending idiot Velu. They can be housemaids like Janet, or special friends like our Boy's friend. They are all the same.

Now you know why I hate their kind. People like them are the ones who do all the fighting. They burn houses, throw bombs and kill soldiers like my brother Jaya who was only guarding a road. They broke my little world and made a poor person like my mother light lamps for her son and pray and cry every night.

That's what I wanted to tell my Master's daughter.

But, I just didn't know how.

The Girl

The river house got quiet again. The holidays were over. The special tree we made for the man who gave us gifts was taken to pieces and packed again into a big bag. We took all the little angel dolls, the silent bells and the shining balls and carefully wrapped them in half sheets of newspaper before arranging them neatly in old shoeboxes. We were careful; we didn't want to break any. The Girl was in charge of all this. She was good at this kind of thing.

'When Christmas comes again, we will take them out to make another tree.' That's what she told me.

I didn't know why we had to take all that trouble to wrap and pack if we had to make that tree again. We could just leave everything as they were. The house looked nice with the tree, the balls shining, the angel dolls rolling with the wind and the silent golden bells not disturbing anyone.

Most times my thoughts did not agree with what the Girl had in mind. For that matter, they seldom agreed with what most people had in mind.

The house lost the cake smell and became the normal river house. The visitors slowly reduced and then stopped coming. The usual ones still came, like Raji Sir and Velu's Master and Madam and a few others who were friends of the family. The Boy and the Girl had some more days left before it was time for them to go back to school.

The Boy's special friend went off to some other country where her parents were living. She gave us gifts before she left. I also got one. She gave me a shirt. I didn't know what to think of her. The more I hated her, the more she smiled with me. Anyway, I was glad when she left. The Boy and I were once again free to do what we normally did.

Most mornings we wore our hats and went in the boat.

'I'll row Sammy. It's good for my muscles. You just sit and enjoy.' That's what the Boy always said.

So he rowed *Solitaire*, our red boat and I just sat and watched the river.

The morning was a beautiful time to be out there in the open. It was nice and cool in the river and the moist filled breeze was always there, blowing fresh against our faces. The fish leapt out of the water, the gulls flew overhead and the river crawled slowly between the deep green foliage on the river banks which were dotted with all kinds of flowers.

The cormorants, crow like birds the colour of midnight, basked in the sun. They perched on the bamboo poles that sprouted up from the *Ja kotu,* the shrimp traps fencing the river. The black birds would fly off as we came near, land in the water and swim with their heads sticking in and out, as if mocking us. The white cranes too were always there, walking along the river bank, long beaks and longer legs, slow marching and watching patiently, waiting for some stupid fish to come by.

These were the common river scenes. Occasionally we would spot a solitary brown eagle floating in the sky, wings spread wide, just gliding in his loneliness, searching for the glimpse of a ripple in the water, to dive and catch his breakfast.

That's what I saw when I sat in the canoe whilst the Boy rowed to build his arm muscles.

Sam's Story

It was all very beautiful.

My Master had friends who lived by the riverbank. The Boy knew most of them. Sometimes we stopped at their houses. Shibly Sir's house was about a mile down from our place and he was always there standing by the fence wearing his shorts and looking at the river.

The Boy told me he was a big man in the Law though he wore shorts. It is mainly for the weekends he came to his river house. Rest of the time he was talking big things in the law with big people in the city.

Shibly Sir would wave whenever he saw us. The Boy would row the boat to him and stop and talk. He always asked the same questions.

'How are you? When are you going back?' That's how he began with his first lot.

'How's your father? How's your mother? How's everything?' That was his second lot of questions.

I think being a big man in Law, Shibly Sir must be someone who always asked questions.

The Boy would grin and answer him. Then we would row on and Shibly Sir would stand and keep waving as if it was the last time he would see us.

If we went back a day later he would ask the same questions and wave the same way when we left.

Same shorts too.

Sometimes we would go up river, in the opposite direction of Shibly Sir's house. That's when we went to the big lake to pick flowers for our Madam. It was a fair distance away to row, but we didn't mind. It was good for the Boy's muscles. We had to row under the big bridge and then go another long time before we came to the area where the flowers were.

Mr. David's house was there. He was a big businessman. My Master knew him well. My Master knew his son too; the son was a very thin young man who had a pretty white wife. Sometimes we would stop at their house and have tea with them. Mr. David owned a big boat with two motors at the back. He often went fishing to the sea. He had to pass our river house to get to the river mouth. Mr. David sometimes stopped by and invited my Master to go fishing with him. My Master was no fisherman; he never went.

'David doesn't catch anything,' my Master used to laugh loud and say.

'He spends the day in the sea and comes empty. On the way home he stops by the bridge and buys some fish from the mongers and goes and tells his wife he caught them. That's how he becomes a big fisherman,' my Master would mockingly explain.

Just a little past Mr. David's house was where we went to pick flowers. That edge of the lake was very beautiful, a wide sea of colours. That's what the flower-fields in the river looked like from a distance. Red lotuses, white water lilies and bluish purple *manel*, all swaying in the wind, as if put together by some unseen hands of a God in a patternless beautiful floor carpet.

We could pick as much as we wanted. The Boy would row the boat slow and steady and I would lean out and pluck the flowers. We would take our time and fill the boat and then start back home.

When we returned, the vases in the river house would overflow with lotuses, lilies and *manel*.

Madam and Madam's daughter were always happy when we brought them a boat full of beautiful flowers. I used to wish someone would come to the river house on such days. Anyone who came would admire the vases and ask where the flowers were from.

'Sammy boy picked them for me,' my Madam would proudly reply.

'He goes in the boat with my son and picks them from the river.'

That's what she always said, giving me full credit. The Boy already had enough in many other things. He didn't need any flower credit.

'Sam is our flower child,' she used to laugh and add.

The visitors would look at me, I think mostly with awe and I would give them my 'flower child nod' in acknowledgment of their admiration. I would add a grin too, just for greater glory. On such evenings I felt very nice, looking at the vases overflowing with my flowers and being admired by everyone as the flower child of the river house.

The Boy and I would often meet the fishermen in the river when we went out in our boat. They all knew us. The Boy always stopped by the fishermen's little canoes to talk to them. They would be sitting on their ramshackle boats and baiting the fish with their curved home-made fishing rods which at a distance looked like spider legs.

Dickman Maama, Dal Maama and Gamini Aiya, they were the regulars on the river. There were a few others too, but we didn't know their names, only their faces. The fishermen were always there, worming their hooks and swinging their *kitul* rods.

Sometimes they would offer the Boy some fish to take home. Dal Maama always did that. He was an old man who had been fishing all his life. He sometimes came to our house and stood near the gate. My Boss knew why he came. Dal Maama never asked but my Boss never failed to give him a few rupees when he visited the river house.

'The poor man has no one,' my Master used to say.

'His wife died some years back and his son went to jail. The young fellow stabbed someone in some drunken fight.' My Master told us the story of the old man's life.

'He has only the fish now and sometimes they don't bite,' he used to further explain to whoever was there to listen.

Dal Maama always tried to pay back by giving fish to our Boy.

That was the river for you, soft and simple for anyone who cared to love it. The fish jumped, the gulls flew overhead and the sky changed colours from sunrise to sunset. Dal Maama and his clan waited patiently, along with the cormorants and the cranes for the fish to become foolish. The river flowed with wind swept waves, sometimes slow, sometimes fast, passing the people who stood by the bank and watched the way the water danced.

Same things, same birds, same faces.

Just like Shibly Sir's questions, no change.

Then there were the Boy and I and *Solitaire* our long red boat. He rowing to build his arm muscles and I sitting with my hat on, watching the pictures and the pleasantries of the river that always remained the same.

It was nothing much, but it was a lot too, at least to me.

I would never forget those times in the river no matter how long and fast the years rolled and how old I became. The simple things I saw and the simple things the Boy and I did with our boat, enjoyable and beautiful.

I'm glad I had them. These were real good times, perhaps the best. I am always grateful that there were a few pleasant things that happened in my life, like my river stories. They are so nice to remember, far too nice to forget. They would remain with me forever.

Sam's Story

When everyone was home in the river house everything was peaceful. Leandro never spoke about his war and he stopped giving his chicken laughs with Janet. They left me alone. I was too busy even to notice them. He was too busy too, doing his stupid cooking and Janet was always arranging the house and helping Madam to keep it neat. The days passed lazily, each of us busy doing our own things. It was a good change after the rush of Christmas.

It was during this time that I got a lot of practice answering the telephone. When the Boy and the Girl were at home the telephone never stopped ringing. Their friends called often. I was the one who answered the phone and told them to 'hold line'. That's what the Girl taught me to say, 'hold line', and then I had to run and give the phone to the Boy or the Girl. It was a good thing that this telephone had no wire. You could even take it to the garden and talk.

The Girl was always trying to teach me things. The problem was I didn't know to write. Everything she said I had to remember. That was very difficult. Somehow I found it difficult to keep things in mind, to remember them. I could remember some things when I first heard, but when someone asked, I forgot. That was the problem, the recalling part.

She also tried to teach me things in English and how to say this and that and what to say when people spoke to me. But I think sometimes I got my lines mixed up and often confused whoever I was talking to.

Of course there were a few times they understood some things I said. Then they always said 'Sam, well said or Sam well done.' I loved to hear those 'well' words, mainly because it didn't happen very often.

The Girl taught me other things too, to say 'please' and 'thank you' and little words like that. She said that is how gentlemen spoke.

'I'm trying to make a gentleman out of you Sammy,' she often said in a serious note when she taught me these words in English.

I didn't know what she meant. But I realised it wasn't going to be that difficult to become a good gentleman; simply a matter of knowing some words and learning how to speak them.

Sammy the gentleman, it did sound nice, better than Sammy the bar hawk or Sammy the airport bat.

The other things I learnt were names of different colours; red, green, white, blue and black. The car was red, the sky was blue and all the nights were black, things like that. She told me the leaves were green and the cranes were white, so were clouds and cotton-wool – pure clean white.

She also taught me the names of numbers, one, two, three, five, nine twenty and so on. I don't think I was very good with numbers. I only knew two thousand. That was the year and I always said twenty-five when anybody asked my age. I didn't really know what they meant; I just liked the way they sounded. Beyond these two, any other number was meaningless to me.

The girl of course would never give up. Bad enough I couldn't figure what numbers were all about; she even tried to teach me to count them. It was easy for her to say what is five and four and things like that. But I could never understand what she meant, how two numbers put together became one number. After some very stubborn attempts, I think she gave up.

I also learnt from her what to ask when I served drinks to visitors. That one was easy, not confusing like numbers.

'Cool or not cool? scott or beer?' easy.

Sam's Story

It was mainly the tea and the coffee that sometimes gave me trouble. Everyone who came to the river house was very fussy about how they drank their tea and coffee. Some drank with sugar, some, no sugar, some, half sugar, little milk, lot of milk, no milk, so many different ways. I had to ask how each one wanted their drink and then remember.

'Tea or coffee?'
'Sugar, shu nogger?'
'White or blue?' That's how I asked

At times they laughed. I didn't know why but I had a feeling I mixed things up. I'm sure those laughs had something to do with the way I took their tea orders.

Velu's daughter became a woman and Velu went home to his village in the hill country to celebrate.

Even in our village it was a big thing when a girl became a woman. You always told the whole world about what happened and made a celebration. Velu celebrated and never came back.

Mr. Gunasekera was a bit disappointed. I heard him tell that to my Master.

'He could have at least told us he wasn't coming,' that's what he said to my Boss.

I always knew that this Velu was a slimy one and would go without telling anyone. I never liked him, specially the way he bent in two and grinned like a fool whenever my Master spoke to him.

'You never know,' my Master said to Mr. Gunasekera. 'He may have been a spy planted here to give information. With this war, anything is possible.'

The days after that Christmas, when the year was 2000, most people often spoke about the war. There were two things that our people liked to talk about. Cricket matches between our country and other countries and the war in the north. Everybody loved talking about cricket. They hated the war, but still spoke so much about it. That's all they spoke of. Like or hate didn't matter.

When there were matches, everybody forgot everything else and spoke only of who played and who shouldn't play and who took money to lose matches and who were honest to play real cricket.

When the matches were over, they went back to their usual talk, which was always about the war.

Of course anytime people spoke about anything the ending was the same. They never failed to say bad things about our leaders who ruled the country. That was common to any conversation.

'Pal Horu machan' that's how they began, and then went for additions like *'Boru Karayo'* and *'Pissu Yakku'* all to describe the people who were supposed to be our leaders in our government. Then they made the final curse. "*Unta henagahanna ona'* which was the worst they wished, asking the gods to send lightning to strike them down.

'When did they tell the truth? The question was the most common. 'They always lie. No matter what colour they wear, it is the same story. Most of them are there to look after themselves and all their catchers. So how can the country progress?' That's what everybody always said.

It was funny how anything bad or troublesome was instantly connected to the leaders. When it rained too much, they blamed the leaders. When it didn't rain, they still blamed the leaders.

I guess when things go wrong people always look for someone to blame. Even when our cricket team lost their cricket matches, people blamed the defeats on the leaders who were running the country.

In that first month of 2000 there were no cricket matches. I remember that because it was the time when Velu's daughter became a woman and Velu became a spy. So the subject was always the war. It didn't matter who you were or where you were, the talk was always the same.

In Lucky's barber shop, people spoke of the war whilst they waited their turn to get their haircuts. When we stood in line for our bread in muscle Menda's bakery, it was the same. The topic never changed. When Harrison and I took the car for servicing we had to wait long. We sat on the wooden bench under the jam fruit tree that shaded the petrol-shed yard. There were others too who were there, chewing betel or roguishly smoking their cigarettes whilst waiting their turn to get their cars cleaned. It was always a long wait; so we spoke and all we said was about the war.

'We heard this,' 'We heard that,' 'I was told this,' 'I saw this with my own eyes after the bomb went off' – this kind of talk was always common. Each one giving his version of what was happening in the country because of the war. I am sure there were a lot of lies said too. At least if they were not lies, they were sure exaggerations. But, it was war talk, always the war talk. Whenever people gathered they spoke of the miserable war.

The river house was no different. When visitors came in the evening to meet my Master and Madam, the conversation at most times turned towards the north and went to the war.

The fighting had increased and the bombs were everywhere. One exploded in a railway station in Colombo and killed a lot of innocent people. The newspapers and the television programs were full of the violence that was erupting in the country; all to do with the war. I never could read the papers and I rarely looked at the television, but I heard them talk.

Most of the river house visitors had their own versions, each one giving his or her expert opinion about how the problem could be solved. None of them had been in the war, or for that matter, none of them had anyone from their families who were involved in the fighting. The real conflict was far from them. But they talked; they always spoke as if they had all the answers.

I listened to everything they said. I was most times there standing on the side, waiting to make drinks for them and refill their fast emptying glasses.

'No point talking about all this,' that's how the conversation started. Always the same beginning, then they went on for hours arguing the 'no point' talk.

'This is one hell of a mess,' that was my Master's usual contribution whenever he spoke of the war. 'I'm glad my children are not here. One of these days I will also pack up and go off. This place is going to the dogs.'

'For you, it is easy,' that was Pradeep Sir. He was the large man who came often to the river house in his big car.

'We have to stay here and take all the shiit,' he always spoke in anger when the war subject came up. I think he liked this word shit; he used it all the time, whenever he said anything. It was not like others, the way he said the word. He dragged, like 'shiit', that's what he said, sounded like the sheet covering the bed in my Boss' bedroom.

'They are increasing the taxes again. They need the money to buy their shiit arms and we pay. For what?' He would ask whoever was there, and then give the answer himself. 'For them to drive their shiit BMWs and leave enough shiit dollars for their generations to come.'

'I tell you man; this is a load of shiit. What they should do is to give the damn thing and put an end to this shiit war, so that we can all live in peace and get on with our lives.'

That was his opinion, the shiit opinion. This was always followed by a quick gulp; one less is-scotch for my Boss' bottle.

'You cannot separate a country like that Pradeep.' That was Velu's master, Mr. Gunasekera. He was always the quiet one in any conversation. He had also been affected by the war. His spy had gone off and there was no one to feed Duke, his dog and take him for his daily walk. Worse, he had no one to bring the bread in the morning and attend to all the errands in the Gunasekera house when he and his madam went to work. That was his problem. The war had directly affected him.

'How can you draw a line and divide a country?' he raised his hand and cut the air to give action to his argument. 'What will happen to all their people who are living on our side? Do you think they would like to give up everything they have and go to the north to live in their new homeland?' Mr. Gunasekera's questions came one after the other, like a little knowing eager schoolmaster dealing with ignorant little school children.

'I don't know, maybe that's what they should do,' Pradeep Sir answered. He had only one solution, divide and give, one part to them, one part to us.

'That will never happen,' Raji Sir voiced. 'You cannot tell people just to pack and go. This has been their home for hundreds of years. You can draw lines and divide the country. But, can you do that to people? Whatever the reasons maybe?'

'Then what is the solution?' that was Pradeep Sir again, minus his shiit business.

'How do I know?' replied Raji Sir.

'That is the problem. Nobody in this country knows the answers,' Mr. Gunasekera made a wise statement.

'We all talk about it. We question and criticize, we have our ideological feuds and then we forget. We wait for the next bomb to explode in Colombo or the next big battle to take place in the north to ask our questions again. We get no answers. We know there are no answers. So we forget the questions and swallow the criticism and go back to talking cricket or whatever we saw about the world on CNN. Isn't that what it had been for the last fifteen years?'

Nobody answered him. I think they knew he was right. There was no opposition, no argument to offer.

'I'll tell you how this war can be stopped,' Raji Sir spoke through a mouthful of potato chips.

'They must make some drastic changes. They must forget all the political bullshit and their personal differences and unanimously address this problem,' the words came out with a spraying of potato crumbs mixed with his new-found wisdom.

'Just see what is happening,' he pointed his index finger at his audience like a politician and took centre stage.

'Most of the soldiers fighting on our side are from the villages. Poor boys who have no employment and go to war to find some money to feed their families,' he explained.

'They have no jobs in this country. So they go to fight and they die. Their parents are too poor to even understand what is happening, let alone protest. That is the untold story of most of our soldiers. The situation is super simple for all of us to accept. The war goes on, the poor die and the rich get richer and the rest of us enjoy watching cricket matches or tele-dramas. The only way this war will stop is if the stupid bastards who are making the decisions wake up and find some solution. It must be something different to what they have been doing for the last fifteen years.'

'So what is the thing they can do differently?' Mr. Gunasekera asked.

Sam's Story

Raji Sir didn't answer immediately. He took his time. He wasn't going to solve the country's problem that quick. He munched some more potato chips before continuing.

'They must make military service compulsory for all the young men,' he said in a serious tone, his voice going soft like a temple priest's.

'Then only you can see the real fun. When the dying reaches the rich and the powerful,' he gave a funny rumbling laugh and went on.

'That will be the only time there will be serious considerations about how to end the war. Till that happens, this sick business will go on. For us, there is no battle. We all wash our hands. It is the poor who are there. It is their war and their sons. They are the ones fighting to stop people from dividing our country so that your tomorrow and my tomorrow will be secured.'

'Am I not right?' he asked directly from my Master.

My Master didn't answer. He just nodded and took a long sip from his glass and looked at our Boy who was seated in the far corner, looking at some magazine.

I don't think my Master would have allowed the Boy to go to war; to guard a stupid road or sit in a lorry full of soldiers and go looking for the enemy.

Our Boy knew very little about the war and what was going on. He only came here for holidays. To jump in the river and send his skyrockets, or row the red boat to build his arm muscles. This war had nothing to do with him. He was out of it, protected by who he was.

The sad part is my two little brothers didn't know about the war either. They certainly had nothing to do with it.

But then, they didn't have anyone to protect them. They had no skyrockets to send or red boats to row or arm muscles to build. They had no father to send them off to school in a far away land, or to speak to someone to keep them out of the war.

For that matter, they didn't have anybody to even call their father.

That's why Jaya and Madiya went to this miserable war, one to die, the other to run and hide and be called a coward, whilst the Boy went to a far away school to learn how to become a big man.

It was difficult for me to understand what life was all about. So different for so many of us, with none of us having any clear answers to all the questions we had.

My Madam never joined in the war conversation. She just sat there; eyes wide open, turning her head like a garden lizard, from one speaker to the other, depending on who spoke. My Madam on rare occasions did add her version. Our Madam's words were simple, just mother's words.

'They are all someone's children, aren't they? Some poor mother who sees her son going to fight for no reason and gets killed in a war in which they had nothing to do. What difference does it make what race they belong to? Or for that matter who they are? The sadness is the same. Is there anything sadder than having to stand and shed tears while they bury your son?

'It is absurd and it is very sad.' That was the sum total of my Madam's contribution.

Most days, the evening conversations in the river house went on along these lines; long loud arguments and absurd solutions, all about the war, given by people who had absolutely no knowledge or any connection to it. I just poured their drinks, refilled their glasses and listened to everything the experts said.

Sometimes these talks lasted well into the late hours of the night and spilled out even to the gate till they got into their cars. No one left in a hurry; everyone got up to go and lingered long.

'That is the Sri Lankan good-bye Sammy,' the Boy once told me. 'From the seats to the verandah, from the verandah to the garden and from the garden to the gate, all small stops and small talk.'

These lingering Sri Lankan good-byes sometimes dragged almost to an hour.

I was always there at these evening gatherings; from the first car that came to the river house to the last car that left. From the first drink I poured to the first visitor to the closing of the gates. My ears always wide open to hear everything they said which at most times I thought was nonsense.

The war in the north was always there. The fighting had been going on for such a long time that the whole country had got used to it. There was always the war to talk about. It had almost become a way of life for people to give their views about the war and connect everyone and everything to it.

That is why when that fool Velu went for his daughter's woman celebration and didn't return, the reason was immediately connected to the war. Another time, people would have thought that he had gone to the village and got drunk, or maybe had got another job. That's what people would have said.

But now it was a different story. The stupid slimy half-bending Velu had become a spy. It wasn't us; it was the miserable war. Sometimes they would show in the television about the fighting that was going on in the north. There were times I watched, especially when they were showing pictures about the men who were in our military.

They showed our soldiers sitting on top of large vehicles with a large gun sticking out and going about shooting the enemy. They always wore little branches of trees on their hats and wore clothes the colour of dried leaves. I wasn't interested in them, but I thought maybe our little one had gone back to the war and maybe he will be in a picture.

I always looked carefully at the soldiers hoping to see Madiya. He was never there.

It was stupid of me to keep looking. He couldn't be in the war again. I remember how he swore that he will never go back to fight. He said he would die before that happened.

Sometimes they showed the other side too. They never went in big vehicles with big guns jutting out. They only rode bicycles, thin black boys wearing sarongs and sleeveless *baniyam* and carrying heavy guns with belts of ammunition. They didn't even have shoes to wear to go to war. Most of them were little boys and some of them were young women like our Janet.

Whenever the other side was shown Janet went silent and kept looking at the pictures. I think she too was searching, the same as I did.

Her little brother too had left home to fight the war.

In a way, both Janet and I were creating our own hopes without admitting they were hopeless. Though we never spoke about it, I think we both knew that neither of us would ever see our little brothers again.

That was the strangeness about all this.

Here was Janet and I, one cleaning the river house and the other switching lights and watering the garden and both of us eating the same food seated in the same kitchen. We even shared the same toilet. That was one moment. The next, we were both searching for our brothers in the television pictures.

Sam's Story

They were fighting a war on separate sides, a war they never wanted to fight. They probably didn't even know why they were fighting.

I used to sometimes wonder why I couldn't understand what this war was all about. At times I thought maybe it was because I was a little different. Maybe that was the reason why I couldn't figure out what was happening and why people were killing each other. I mean this war in the north and this business of dividing our country; one side to Leandro and Janet and their people and one side for us. It was too complicated, but I had no one to ask. That's why I thought that this war must be something very special. People like me couldn't understand. Never mind me, it was even beyond people like my Master and his friends to make any sense of it.

If none of us didn't know what this was all about, then, there must have been some very special reasons for this war.

I don't think those who knew the reasons and kept the war going ever fought in the battles.

It was left for others, poor boys like Jaya and Madiya and Janet's missing brother to do the fighting and die.

Come to think of it, I think Raji Sir was right. Even I could see that he had a point.

This war seemed certainly a poor man's war, at least where the dying was concerned. Only the poor died and had nice military funerals. The rest of the people in the country gave money or took money and sat in their chairs and gave opinions.

The fighting and the dying were mainly left to young boys and girls who were poor and had no powerful fathers. They were the ones who went about carrying their guns, some sitting on big wheeled vehicles with bigger guns and some pedalling their stupid bicycles, each looking for the other to fight and kill.

All these young men and women were buried and forgotten no sooner than they had shed their blood.

That was the war for you, thousands on both sides dying their causeless deaths, totally meaningless, no matter to which side they belonged.

I think it must be some real stupid war.

Everyone

The Boy and Girl left the river house and went back to the far away country, back to where their learning school was. They would return again only in the middle of the year. That's what the Boy told me when he left.

'Fun times are over Sammy boy, it's back to school and back to work.'

The river house became very busy as the day came close for the Boy and the Girl to leave. Madam got Leandro to make special food for the children to take with them.

'I don't want my babies to starve,' she kept repeating.

The food was packed in plastic bags and sealed and pasted with tape, just to make sure they stayed fresh. There were all kinds of food, fried chicken, roasted meat, dried fish, *seenisambal*, you name it and it was there. All kinds of sweets too were packed. Milk toffee, love cake, treacle dripping *kattabibikkan* and many more, anything the Madam thought would take the fancy of her babies.

The way our Madam loaded food I really thought that the school did not have anything to eat at all!

'What nonsense Sammy, there is a lot of food there,' that's how the Boy explained when I asked.

'It's just that she still thinks we are babies and will go hungry unless we take what Leandro makes.'

Janet too got very busy as the departure day came close. She washed and ironed all the clothes, both the Boy's and the Girl's and placed them neatly folded in the suitcases. Our Janet was very good at such things. She was always the neat one, ironing and packing were what she did best.

Madam made lists of all that the Boy and the Girl had to take and ticked each item as they were put in their bags. Our Madam tried very hard to be normal but we all knew she was very very sad. Her babies were leaving. The river house was never the same for her without the children. The last few days she made everything the Girl and the Boy liked to eat, feeding them from morning till night, as if they were never going to see food again.

When the day to depart came near, everyone in the river house was talking and laughing with a great effort to keep things happy. But the pauses were many and they always said in their silence how sad the good-bye was going to be.

The children left exactly three months after they came. I am not so sure about counting these days and months. I am only telling you what they told me. They said it was three months, so it must be three months.

It was one of the happiest times I can remember in my life. So many things happened and almost all of them were things that made me happy. I never could have got enough of it. I never laughed so much and I never ate so much food in my whole life. Except for that special friend business, everything that happened was a happy thing. We ate, we laughed, we made Christmas trees, we went in the boat, we went in the car, we spoke English, and so many things.

It was simply the best time that I could ever remember.

I will never forget them, the good times I had when the our Boy and the Girl were there with me spending their school holidays in the river house.

Sam's Story

Harrison, Leandro and I loaded the bags to the van and Janet made sure the soft bags were placed in a manner not to crush the soft food they carried. There were so many bags; one would think the Boy and the Girl were leaving the river house forever. We all came near the gate and said our final good-byes. My Master and Madam were going with Harrison to the airport to drop the children. This good-bye was for the three of us, Leandro, Janet and me.

'Sammy my friend, you take good care of yourself,' that's what the Boy said. That's how he always spoke to me. I was his friend. I liked when he said things like that and called me his friend.

'You let me know if you need anything Sammy and I'll make sure I will send it to you.'

I didn't need anything. I only needed him to come back soon so that we could do our things together. I knew I was going to miss him very much. But I didn't want to tell him. I didn't want him to feel bad about going away.

'You must look after our boat and you must look after our dogs.'

That is the other thing I liked about this Boy. It was always our boat and our dogs. He knew exactly what belonged to whom. He knew I was also a part owner of all these things we shared, even though I hadn't paid for them. He didn't pay either; it was his father, the Master who paid for everything. But, we were the ones who loved them, the dogs, the boat and such things.

Come to think of it, I think who owns what had more to do with love than who paid for them.

The Girl too said her good-bye to me and as usual had tears in her eyes. She of course was always a bit stupid, only interested in making me say her 'please' and 'thank you' and all those confusing English words. Her life's joys were mainly about how to pour drinks and twist wine bottles and which side the napkins should be kept on the dinner table. That was her world and she did do her best to make me a part of it.

'Sammy, you must study your English.'

I knew it was coming and I was ready. I gave her my special all-purpose grin that meant nothing and everything about anything.

'Don't forget what I taught you. You must remember to practise your English.'

I nodded and kept grinning. That was the best answer; it always worked well when you didn't want to say anything.

We said our good-byes, the three of us to the Boy and the Girl. Janet and the Girl both cried. Leandro of course was too stupid even to know what was happening and kept grinning like a fool when everybody else was very serious. We all said so many things to each other, all speaking at the same time, reciting like talking parrots the meaningless words that come out from people when they say good-bye and go away from each other.

The Girl hugged Janet, then Leandro and then me; she was like that, very soft. She didn't mind hugging us, the house servants. The Boy was too tough for all that. He just patted my shoulder and rolled his open palm on my head, his fingers crawling all over my hair. I kept looking down, afraid to talk, more afraid that he will see the wetness that was all over my cheeks.

'Look after yourself.'
'Take good care.'
'Look after the old couple.'
'Come back soon.'
'Don't forget to eat the cake.'
'Leandro, cook well.'
'Sammy, clean the boat.'

Sam's Story

'Janet, make sure your hair is combed and oiled.'

All those parting words spilled out from us, one after the other and all together, mostly in whispers. What each one said was choked with emotion and was drowned in the confusion of getting into the van with hands patting and touching in farewell. Everything was shadowed by the sadness that spread among us, equal in distribution, deflating all of us and defeating our best attempts at acting normal.

It was indeed a sad farewell.

I even told them to send me a letter, as if I could read.

We watched the van start up and go off. It sped away from the river house out in a cloud of dust with its horn blaring. That was Harrison's way of saying the last good-bye.

Harrison was in front and the family was seated in the back, the Master, alone in one seat and our Madam, in motherly comfort, seated between her two babies.

The van turned right, leaving our little street to join the main road that would go past the town and on to the airport, which was two hours away.

The three of us kept waving till they took the turn and disappeared.

Only then did I realise how lonely and sad it would be, to go back to the empty river house.

Life settled to the normal slow pace. The fast times were temporarily over. The Boy and the Girl were far away and the river house became quiet. Only the weekends became busy, especially Friday nights when my Master's friends came to the river house to drink and eat and solve the country's problems. Other than that the normal days just came and went in a lazy mood.

Most fridays we ate hoppers for dinner. That was Madam's plan.

'Don't know who will come, better be prepared.'

We didn't cook them. Once Leandro tried and his hoppers became brown and broken, more like *pol-leli,* dried coconut husks. Even Bhurus refused to eat them. That is why every Friday Harrison and I went in the van to bring hoppers.

We bought them from the hopper woman who had a stall near the beach. I don't know what to call her, woman or man. Everybody called her 'Bilin Kajja.' They say she was a man before and then became a woman. That maybe true because I often noticed she spoke in a rough voice and had a lot of hair on her arms and legs. She had a little moustache too and she always walked funny, kind of rolling her arse purposely to show she is a woman. Bilin Kajja made good hoppers, crisp, nice and rounded; they were real hoppers, not like Leandro's broken coconut husks.

Whenever we mentioned her name everybody laughed. It took me a while to figure out what the joke was all about. You have to read the name in reverse, then only the laughs are explained when 'Bilin Kajja' becomes 'Kalin Bijja'.

Now that was someone's clever idea.

'Kalin Bijja'- the one who had balls before. That was clever.

Bijja or no Bijja, whatever her name was, one thing was sure. She was the world champion hopper maker. I must tell you that what she hid between her legs had nothing to do with the way she made her wonderful hoppers. They were the best. She was indeed the world champion.

Every Friday Harrison and I bought a basket full of hoppers, egg hoppers and plain hoppers and Leandro made the curries at home with a *pol sambole* for added flavour. When Friday nights came we were ready for any amount of visitors who dropped by for dinner. Leandro's curries and sambol and Bilin Kajja's hoppers was a favourite meal among my Master's friends.

After a few beers and a few Russians they all ate hoppers and sat around to solve the country's problems till late in the night.

Gamini Aiya, the fisherman, came with a list to collect money.

Old Dal Maama had died. He went to sleep and never woke up. Dal Maama had nothing to leave for anybody other than his ramshackle dugout canoe and his home-made *kitul* fishing rods.

His son was still in jail. Dal Maama had no one to call family to bury him. The fishermen of the river had got together and were collecting money to give him a decent burial. Pity, Dal Maama was not in the military. He would have got a real nice funeral like my brother Jaya did, with speeches from military-men and biscuits and drinks for the people who came to bury him.

My Master went to the funeral and took me along. All the fishermen were there, Gamini Aiya and a few others who I didn't know by name.

Dal Maama's best friend old Dickman was there too. He was also a very old man. I think he himself was getting ready to go. Must have come to see how it was all done.

I was surprised to see some women wailing and tearing their hair and crying loud. They rolled on the ground and croaked like frogs when the coffin was lowered. I thought Dal Maama didn't have any family.

'Don't be stupid Sam, they are not his family,' my Master made me wise. 'They have been hired to cry, that is why they are so loud,' he explained. 'If I die, don't forget to hire some women to do the crying,' he grinned at me and added.

There were only a few people there at the cemetery. Dal Maama was buried where the poor people were buried; the vacant plot behind the school where the fishermen's children went to learn. This was no real cemetery with marble doll angels and cement-slab name boards. Just an empty land that had a few broken wooden crosses sticking out of the ground to show where someone was buried. Most graves were simply swollen earth, no remembrance; no one to remember.

That was the poor for you; even in death they clearly carried their miserable mark.

That's how it all ended for Dal Maama.

Became old beyond his years wasting his life in the river. Dugout canoe with bent homemade fishing rods and spent his days in the sun and rain hoping to make the fish foolish. Borrowed money from my Master and paid back with fish.

What a life.

We all threw some sand into the hole to cover the coffin.

The hired women were still crying.

The war in the north went on and on. Nobody seemed to care much. So many villages got burnt and bombed on both sides. People became homeless, children went hungry, people died and no one bothered. At least once a month a bomb went off in some big city and killed a few innocent people. When something like that happened for a few days everyone spoke about it and said how sad it all was. Then they forgot.

There were other things to think about. Life went on.

The war was there in the far north and we were here in the towns. That was all there was to it in everyone's mind. As long as nobody known died, no one cared.

With time, even Leandro lost his interest to scare me with his war talk. Velu was long gone after his daughter's woman celebration. There was no one for Leandro to talk about his war. Janet was not very keen to know what happened in the north.

I also lost interest to hate him. Sometimes when we were in the room we spoke and said things to each other. He once even asked me what I like to eat so that he can cook that for me. Between the two of us the hatred slowly reduced, only a little jealousy remained. That had nothing to do with the war. It was more to do with Janet.

Leandro and I shared the same room. I guess we got used to each other.

Often the government bosses came on the television to tell us about the war. They always boasted that everything would be over in one month.

'We have the best guns to fight the war. We have bought the best equipment for our soldiers to kill the enemy. It will all be over soon. Not more than a month to finish them all and bring peace to the whole country.'

It was one very long month that never saw an end.

There were always so many stories about how the war was going on. I heard this talk every time I went to the market. Them winning and us winning, news like that. Sometimes there were more details. Some road taken and some town lost and some boats sunk in the sea or some aerobblane crashed in the jungle. There was always the count of how many were killed and how many bodies were collected and how many ended up without arms and legs in hospitals.

The real truth I think was that both sides were losing. But nobody wanted to say that.

I was too busy to worry about what was happening in the north and who was winning and who was losing the war. I had my hands full with watering the garden and attending to the million things in the river house that our Madam had entrusted me to do. In any case, my dealings with the war were long over.

It was finished a long time ago, when I lost my two brothers.

Some thieves broke into Lucky's barbershop.

I always knew this Lucky was unlucky; never mind his name. They had come to steal things from Tee Malli's vegetable shop and may have thought why not go up the steps and take what was in the salon. They should have known when they climbed the poor half steps that this was a poor barber man with nothing but some brushes and combs and some cheap half empty face powder cans.

They didn't care; they took everything including his two and only cassette music.

That was the day both Tee Malli and our unlucky Lucky joined my club, the poor club.

'I am going back to my village,' that's what the barber told my Boss when he went to see him. We heard about the robbery and went to see for ourselves. The thieves had taken everything including Lucky's half dirty wall mirror.

There was an empty space where Lucky's mirror used to hang.

There was an empty man where Lucky had been.

Tee Malli of course was looking for revenge.

He had gone to the local police to complain and the police had come and tried to find the thieves. It was all in vain; they could not find anybody. Those thieves must have already eaten all the vegetables and must have been powdering their rogue faces and combing their hair with Lucky's combs and brushes.

Sam's Story

'I know where to go, I'll teach those bastards a lesson,' Tee Malli boasted, somewhat in a foolish manner, maybe to curb his frustration.

'I know a place where I can break a coconut and curse those thieving bastards. They will end up losing their limbs, maybe even dead.'

Tee Malli was not happy with the town police and the local law. He was taking his case to the gods themselves. I always thought that the gods were very busy. I didn't know that they had time to catch vegetable thieves and break their arms and legs because Tee Malli broke a coconut.

All in all it was we who lost. We lost our place to buy our beetroot and carrot and my Boss and I had to find a new barber to cut our hair and a new way to find out the latest things that happened in the town.

Tee Malli never opened his vegetable shop again. Instead he became an agent to a bookie and collected horse race bets. I think he is now doing well. He now goes in a 'Chally'; those dwarf scooters that everybody rides these days. No more beetroot carrot nonsense. He had found his way to money with horses and other people's hopes and pains.

I heard Harrison say that our unlucky Lucky went back to his village. It was in the hills, a far away place. His family too was like Tee Malli; they were in the vegetable business. They didn't sell, but they grew vegetables. Lucky went to help his father cultivate cabbage.

Lena had dog babies. One died at birth, one died a day later and two survived. We were all excited about the new arrivals at the river house.

'Sammy, now you are an uncle,' Madam laughed and said. 'They are called puppies Sam, Lena's puppies.'

'Uncle Sam,' that sounded the best. Better than gentleman Sam or even better than Hawk-like Sam or Sam Bat who ran like a bat out of hell.

Of course everybody knew who the father was. The little ones came with ugly mouths and pug noses and looked even uglier than Bhurus.

Janet and Madam were the extra mothers. I was the uncle. For one whole week nothing happened in the river house other than puppy business. Madam even telephoned the Boy and the Girl to tell them about Bhurus and Lena's children.

Everybody who came to the river house wanted to see the puppies and everyone was making their bids to Madam to get one. Some even said we could sell them.

'They are expensive; you can make a lot of money. This kind of puppies are hard to come by.'

Madam never sold them. I was glad. They were my friend's children. I was their uncle and I sure didn't want anybody selling my two nephews. Both puppies were given to Velu's Madam.

'She loves dogs Sam; she'll take good care of them. That's why I want to gift them.' Madam assured me there was no sale. Velu's madam of course came and made the biggest fuss. She patted Bhurus and Lena and told them she would look after their babies well. She promised to bring them back to visit the parents.

'Don't worry Lena, I'll take good care of them.' She felt Lena's head and assured her.

She promised so many other things too; to brush and bathe them and powder them and to raise them well. She promised everything she could think of. I thought by the way she was going on that she might even promise to send them to church and teach them to pray to their God to make them go to his heaven.

Velu's madam brought nice clean pink sheets to wrap the puppies and a nice decorated wicker basket to carry them home.

Uncle Sam silently watched the whole charade. All the goodbyes and the kisses and the fuss Velu's madam made when she took the puppies away. Those little dogs didn't know anything from nothing or what the hell was happening. Bhurus I think was quite happy to get rid of them to get some attention for himself. The way he was looking at Lena, he probably was already making plans to start work on another set.

Everybody these days was talking about what was happening in the country.

'No money at all, economy is finished, we are ruined,' that's what they all said.

'All the money is going to the war,' that was the next line that followed.

'Very soon this country will not have any money to do anything. We are becoming beggars.'

'Everything has gone up in price, where's the money to buy?'

This is the kind of thing that was in everyone's mouth.

It was beyond me to understand what this no money business was all about. I knew what it was to be poor. Back in the village we have always been poor. My whole family were "poor experts". I mean we had been like that all our life and knew a lot about what it is to be real poor. We ate poor, we slept poor and we lived poor. We certainly knew what it meant to be dirt poor.

I couldn't imagine someone like my Master becoming poor, not with all the things he had. There was no way he would walk along the river bank and pick *gotukola* and *kankun* and bring them home for our Madam to cook. Now that is poor for me. I couldn't see him without the comforts of his fancy home; the fans in his rooms, the cooling boxes in the kitchen overflowing with food. What about his toilet? Would he ever shit or piss on the riverbank, or for that matter would he know how to sell his rice coupons to buy sugar?

When these people spoke of being poor and the country having no money, I don't think they really knew what they were talking about.

This kind of 'no money' talk I mainly heard when I went to the town to buy things with Harrison. People said they had no money and they always cursed.

'Everything is so very expensive child, how to manage?' Tthat's what Raji Sir's wife said. She was normally very quiet, but she too was opening her mouth to join the poor parade. But then they both went and bought a special bicycle. I don't know about being special, but to me it was a stupid bicycle with only one wheel. It couldn't go anywhere. How to go anywhere with one wheel? The bicycle was for them to just sit and pedal and watch television.

That's the so-called poor for you.

The newspapers were telling the country that the kerosene prices had gone up. With it everything went up. Vegetables, meat, soda bottles and bus fare, we had to pay more for all these. People's cursing increased. Muscle Menda immediatly raised the price of buns and bread. Even Billing Kajja cursed and raised the price of her hoppers by half a rupee. Said she needed to pay more for the kerosene to keep her fires going. Ranjith who ran the grocery shop cursed too. I couldn't figure out why he cursed because he was the one who was selling his shop things at higher prices.

I think times were becoming hard for everyone and people had accepted cursing as a way of life. Even Harrison cursed. He had nothing much to curse about. My Master looked after him well. But he too had to be in the curse team. Maybe that is why I often heard him curse the road light when it turned red. He must have thought that it would change to green because he cursed.

To be honest I must admit that once or twice this business of cursing got into me too. I had no complaints about anything, but I too ran with the rest of them and did my share of muttering under my breath. I cursed the trees when the leaves fell and I cursed them more when I had to sweep the garden clean.

But then I realised all that was stupid.

The leaves always fell, the tree didn't care whether I cursed or not. I knew I was simply wasting my breath, just like Harrison's curses as he braked and stopped the van when the lights turned red.

The cursing went on. People cursed the government, people cursed the war and people cursed anything that could be cursed. The country, they said, was going to the dogs. Everybody said there was no money. But everybody just went about with their lives just as before.

Sometimes I wished they all became poor; at least for a short time. Then they would know what this business of being poor was all about; I mean, being real poor like my family was.

Secretly I hoped that one day I would catch my Master plucking *gotukola* and *kankun* from the riverbank. It was a very bad thought. I didn't like to think like that. But sometimes it came and went away fast and I must admit that there was a little fun for me just to imagine the boss man standing in the riverbank mud and bending to pick *gotukola* and *kankun* leaves to eat with his coupon rice.

Leandro went back to his village for a few days for a religious festival and Janet became our temporary cook. I did some of her work like cleaning the rooms and wiping the chairs in the sitting room. I even helped her in the kitchen by cutting onions and scraping coconuts. She was nice to be with, especially with that fool out of the way. She smelt nice and she looked nice.

Every year Leandro went home to celebrate his new year. He was the big man there in the village. All his family and relations waited for him to come home with his river house earnings for all of them to celebrate. He must have felt important, wasting all the money he saved and then coming back penniless.

I had a feeling that this time things could improve for me. I was hoping Leandro would not come back. There was always the possibility that he could go to join their army and get killed somewhere. That would not have been a bad thing; I would have had Janet all to myself.

The stupid bastard came back, as usual penniless. I am sure he must have gone and tried to join their army and they would have chased him away. Who would take him, so short, almost like a dwarf?

The only change in him was he had completely shaved his head. Leandro was egg bald like a stunted mushroom and looked even more stupid than before. Janet told me he had to do that to go to his temple. He had done it to please his gods.

I could never figure out how it would make his gods happy to see a 'no hair' mushroom midget coming to the temple to ask things from them.

Perhaps his gods were also a bit like him. I don't want to use the word. I don't want to make his gods angry. You know what I mean.

At one stage I think Janet was worried that Leandro would not come back. I saw the way she smiled when he returned. She must have missed their chicken laughs.

I think it was after he shaved his head and visited his gods that things became better for him. Off and on I caught them alone in the room. That's when I heard the chicken laughs change to moans and grunts. I felt jealous.

He made me promise not to tell our Madam. I was scared. So I kept my mouth shut.

'She is going to go and get married soon,' Leandro explained.

'You see Sam, marriage is like cricket; you need to practise.'

That was all right with me but I sure wished that they would sometimes include me also in the team.

Colombo

That morning was no different to most other mornings except for the big black butterflies. My Master and my Madam were going to Colombo and the usual rush was on.

'Sam polish my shoes, Leandro quickly get me a tea, Sam have you washed the car?' that was the Master, rapid firing at us.

'Janet can you bring that thing to dry my hair? Janet where's my brown leather bag? No time to eat, how about a sandwich?' That's Madam's version, all in one great rush.

There were so many little running errands for Leandro, Janet and me whenever these two went somewhere in the morning.

'Take this and put in the car.'

'Janet can you iron my red dress, the one with the small flowers,' Madam jumped from one instruction to another, like a grasshopper.

'Don't forget the brush,' 'Make sure the umbrella is in the back seat, it might rain.'

It all went on like that including the real last minute things they forgot and only remembered when they got into the car. Those of course we had to run faster and bring quickly as the Master had already started the engine. Any slight delay meant the horn went blaring. I was the one who ran like a bat out of hell taking two stairs at a time to bring what they left back in the bedroom.

We were all quite used to this morning madness whenever our Madam and Master left the house to go to the city.

I closed the gate and waved as they drove off. The rush was over. The car sped out and I turned back to the house.

Something was bothering me. I felt uncomfortable and I didn't know why. Leandro was in the kitchen, cooking, and Janet went back to wipe the glass windows. The butterflies were still there, hovering around the shoe flower bushes.

Big black butterflies, just like the ones I saw at Madam Martell's garden when I got the call to come home.

The day passed lazy, the usual morning things happened and we took care of all that. The phone rang, it always rings all the time. Janet took the calls and wrote down the messages. The postman came and delivered letters. I watered the plants and bathed Bhurus and Lena. Leandro went to the market to bring vegetables.

It was a normal morning in the river house.

I was near my pond feeding the fish when I heard the excitement.

It was Leandro.

I heard him shouting and coming through the gate, jabbering in his language to Janet. She too was asking so many things and they ran to the television to switch it on, to see something that was happening in Colombo.

It took me awhile to get their attention and then it was Janet who told me what this was all about.

'It is a bomb Sam,' Janet whispered. 'A big bomb had gone off in Colombo. They have bombed the bank,' she said in a voice filled with uncertain emotion.

That's what Leandro heard in the market when he was buying vegetables. He came running home. Many people had died. The building had been completely destroyed.

The three of us looked at one another. We were too scared to speak. We didn't know what to say or how to admit.

We all knew that our Madam and Master always went to the big bank whenever they visited the city.

It was all on television and they showed everything that had happened an hour ago and what was happening at that time, lot of confused pictures and a lot of confused people.

There seemed to be chaos everywhere. Policemen were going about blowing whistles and pushing people who were gathering in hundreds to see what was going on. The building was completely broken and still smoking in so many places.

There was a woman in the television with a small loud phone in her hand, talking in an excited voice to all of us watching television. She told so many things so fast. She said it was a lorry that was filled with bombs that had done all this. It had been driven straight into the bank and exploded.

The television showed the injured being taken out of the building. Some in stretches carried by white uniformed hospital men, some hanging on to friends who were helping them.

Some lay on the ground covered with sheets. I think they were dead.

There were a few hospital cars that were being filled by the wounded. Many people walked about as if dazed, blood soaked bandages wrapped around their heads, shirts torn and faces filled with fear. They were all muttering curses at the people who had shattered their lives.

Sam's Story

The television woman came back on screen. She brought a young man to the picture and started asking him questions.

'It was terrible, it was terrible,' he kept repeating in a voice that broke down at every word.

He said he ran out when he heard the noise and managed to escape. He was crying more than talking. He said there were still many people trapped inside the building. It wasn't very clear what he was saying. I think he was still shaking with fear after escaping from the burning building.

A bomb had gone off. People were dead and dying

The hospital cars were running up and down shrieking with their loud horns, carrying the injured. The police were everywhere trying to bring some order to what was happening. They showed all that on television.

Janet, Leandro and I remained silent. We were glued to the television screen as they repeatedly showed the same pictures about the bomb explosion.

Leandro was very quiet. This time it was different to all the other times that bombs had exploded in the city. There was no more boast in Leandro about how great his people were and how many they killed and how stupid my people had become. This bomb was different. We had no war to settle here. We had no winners or losers. There was nothing to boast about and decide who was smart and who was stupid. All that anger and argument we had before whenever anything like this happened had suddenly vanished.

Leandro was silently watching the screen and I was right next to him listening to everything that woman said in the television. I felt Janet clutching my arm and heard the soft sobs of her crying.

Two people we loved very much were supposed to have been there in the bank. We didn't know what had happened to them. We didn't know whether they escaped or whether they were injured. We were so very scared.

The war was no more in the north and there was no more the talk of our soldiers and their soldiers. It was our Madam and our Master. We had no sides to take here. I knew that when I saw the stupid Leandro with tear filled eyes sitting like a fool muttering curses at the people who had bombed the bank.

Suddenly the fighting and the war had become very personal. It had affected people we loved. It had crossed all barriers that divided us and had come like a thief to our river house.

The three of us sat there in the kitchen, shocked and stunned.

It was Janet who decided to act. She was always better than Leandro and me when it came to doing things. She wanted to call somebody to find out. She couldn't just wait. The tension was too much; we were all so very worried.

The telephone lines were busy and no numbers could be reached. I guess everybody was calling each other in Colombo to know what had happened, especially people like us who had someone known who was in the building when the bomb went off.

Janet was trying to get Raji Sir's number and it took her about half an hour of continuous dialing to finally reach him. He knew all about the bomb but he didn't know that our Madam and Master had gone there. Janet said he got very worried when she told him that they had gone to the bank.

'He will call back,' that's what Janet told us.

Sam's Story

We went back again to the television to watch the same pictures of broken people and the broken building and the woman with the loud mike repeating what she said before.

People were still running and carrying the injured. The building was still burning and the hospital cars were going up and down with the shrieking horns, taking the patients to whatever hospitals that were available.

We sat around the kitchen in sombre mood, unable to think and not being sure of what to do. Occasionally we glanced at the television, especially when the woman came back with more news and more new faces that she wanted to interview. A very dark tall big-made police chief came and told the death toll; fifty-four dead and hundreds injured, more deaths to come.

Janet was still crying, softer than before, but still crying. Leandro and I sat silent and confused, each trying to come to terms with what may have happened, each carrying the burden of his own hollow feeling of what could be the unknown.

The butterflies were still hovering around the shoe flower bush. Black patches flying about, just as they did in Madam Martell's garden.

Back to the begining

That is how my story in the river house came to an end.

It was too sad. He didn't have to die.

My Master had nothing to do with this stupid war and nothing against anybody on either side. He had no comment to make about all this business of dividing the country and who should get which part. He only said 'it was all meaningless.' He just drank his Russian and watched his fish eating their green balls and went about carrying people in his aerobblane. That was his life.

He was not a bad man. He didn't have to die, but now he was dead.

The Boy and the Girl came back to bury their father. We were all there and so were many of his friends. They said some nice things about him before they lowered his coffin. But all that was in vain. He was no more, so what good would all the words do.

Leandro cried and Janet cried and I cried too. We all cried. I saw even Harrison cry. When everybody was crying I remembered what my Master told me the day we buried our old friend, Dal Maama. About hiring women to cry when he died. I still remember the way he grinned.

He didn't need any hired criers.

After the funeral all the people lined up to shake hands. The three of them stood at the gate, our Madam hugged by her children. People came by, one by one, to say how sorry they were.

I didn't go.

I didn't know how to begin and what to say. I don't think there were enough words in any language for me to tell them how sad I felt.

The Boy and the Girl took our Madam away.

She went with them to the far country. I heard people say that she never wanted to come back to the river house again. I could understand that. Even I didn't want to go back. It was too sad. That's why I went back to my village.

Leandro and Janet too packed up and left. I don't know where they went. We were all too shattered and confused to do normal things. Nobody asked and nobody told anything. We just went our own ways.

I know Leandro was very sad. He told me that so many times during the days of the funeral.

He never cooked anything. Just sat most times in our room, lying in his camp bed and staring at the ceiling. He loved our Master very much. That's why I saw him cry so much.

'They should not have killed him Sam,' he repeatedly muttered and then mumbled some other things in his own language. It was his people who drove the lorry filled with bombs to the bank and killed our Master. I think he felt bad about that. Somehow it hit him hard, maybe especially because he boasted so many times about how great his people were in this war.

That was the war for you, meaningless, killing people like my Master who had nothing to do with it.

I don't think Leandro wants to join the fighting anymore. He was very sad. I don't think he wants to have anything to do with the war after what happened to the river house. All that big talk about killing my kind dried in him with our Master's death. He told me that before he left. He hugged me too and told me to take care of myself.

'Go home Sam, go back to your village and look after yourself,' that's what he said when he went away.

It is strange how I don't hate him anymore.

I wish we both could go back in time and be in the river house again sharing our small room. Leandro could do his cooking and send all his farts as much as he likes and hang his *lankets* anywhere he wants. We could live there not hating each other; I mean just get on with our stupid lives without worrying about things that are beyond us. No more talking about who is dividing the country and who is winning and who is getting defeated.

It would be nice to do that and have some stupid small fights over who plays cricket matches and who has chicken laughs with Janet.

I could water the plants again and switch the lights on and off and feed green balls to the fish. Bhurus would be there too, so would Lena. I could sit with them in the garden and watch the boats go by and wave at the fishermen. Maybe Leandro, Janet and I could see television together without our stupid democracy and matchstick votes.

I guess there is a lot more to people than how they send their farts and where they hang their multicoloured wet *lankets*. Or for that matter to what kind they belong.

All these thoughts about going back to the river house are good but they are just thoughts. Too many 'maybes', but that is all gone. Even a fool like me can figure that out.

The sad thing is that in the end all our worlds crumbled.

We were all defeated by this stupid war that none of us had anything to do with.

Sam's Story

Now I am back in the village. I sit on my mango tree and often think of the things that happened in my life. There is nothing much to do here. I have a lot of time to just sit and think.

Loku finally got a job in the clothes factory and Podi went to Colombo to be a housemaid like Janet. My mother is too old to tap rubber, but we manage. Life goes on. Our chickens lay big eggs and we still remain good Buddhists eating the *gotukola* and the *kankun* that grow on the riverbank.

Jaya's faded picture still hangs near our door but we don't talk much about him anymore. It has been a long time since the military men came to our village to bury our Jaya. Sometimes we talk about Madiya, Loku and Podi feel the same as I do, but my mother still has hopes that someday the war will be over and our little brother will come home.

We don't like to tell her it might not be so.

Kade Mudalali's shop is still there, along with his book where he writes how much each one owes him. He doesn't scold my mother anymore. Our name is not in the book. We have a little money now to buy our things.

That fool Kaluwa got married to someone who worked in the factory. People in the village said he had to get married. Kaluwa's woman had five brothers who were the rough type. They had come and made it clear to *Kade Mudalali* and Kaluwa that they didn't want any bastard coming out of their sister's belly. That's why Kaluwa had to get married.

Kaluwa's woman is very very ugly; she's got teeth jutting out of her mouth like a banana comb, yellow too and almost straight out of her face. Worst is she is blacker than him. I am waiting to see what their baby will look like, maybe dark blue, maybe like the moonless black midnight, but definitely will be ugly, maybe like a little devil child.

Nothing much has changed in our village. The men still dig sand from the river and drink *kasippu* in the evening to forget their troubles. The women go to tap rubber from the trees and come home to empty kitchens and try to find things to cook their night meal.

I have very little to do with all that is happening in our village. So I mostly sit on my mango tree and try to remember the few nice things that happened in my world.

I often think of the river house.

I have forgotten all the English the Girl taught me, about tea or coffee and how to serve them with milk and sugar or plain black. Those things are not important, just like her folding napkins and twisting the wine bottles. But I rememebr how I got gifts for Christmas and how I ate so much cake.

My best memories I have are the times I spent with the Boy. Things like our red noat and the way he and i went in the river to build his muscles and how we picked flowers for our Madam. I remember many things like that. I feel happy when I think of them, but I feel sad too because they are no more.

It is a pity we cannot bring life back.

I miss my friend Bhurus, I don't think i miss Lena, but I miss Bhurus very much. He was my best friend.

Sometimes I feel like going to see him. I know he would like that. I would like it too. But I feel sad to see him and leave him again. It might break his old heart. I know it would break mine. I think it is better to leave things as they are.

After the river house closed Lena and Bhurus went to live with Velu's Madam. She was very fond of them. They must be alright.

The boy always said taht one day he would come back to the river house to take care of me. I know he meant it. But I don't

Sam's Story

know how it is now. What happened was too sad for all of us. It was Harrison who said they would never return.

'There are too many sorrows for them here Sam, they will never come back.'

I don't know. I wish I knew how they are, especially our Madam. The Boy and the Girl are young and they will learn to live and get on with their lives. It is my Madam that I worry about. She was a good woman. She was always kind to Janet, Leandro and me.

She changed overnight after we buried our Master. She was never the same. She looked kind of old and lost. It is good that she went away. She was too sad.

Sometimes I wish I got a letter from them.

But then, they know I can't read.

Maybe that is why they don't write.

***

A forthcoming book by Elmo Jayawardena
The Last Kingdom of Sinhalay

The advent of the Sinhala people to the island of Lanka dates back to 500 B.C. In 1505 the Portuguese came. Then came the Dutch and the British. In the midst of all the European invasions and the changing of power in the coastal belt Senkadagala, known to the Europeans as Kandy, survived as the last bastion of the Sinhala people.

In 1815 the British invaded the Hill Country and took over Senkadagala. It was never conquered, but was gifted to the British by the Sinhala aristocracy.

"The Last Kingdom of Sinhalay" is the story of the fall of Senkadagala and the brutal realities of greed in colonialism. The story is told through two people, John D'Oyly, an erudite from Cambridge who came to the island as a colonial administrator, and his dear friend, Thera Ihagama, a penniless Buddhist priest turned freedom fighter.

The book tells about the kings and the aristocracy and the conspiracies and the treacheries that took place when men betrayed men to stay in high office. It tells too of ordinary men who rose against the British in revolution to reclaim their land and the atrocious measures taken by the British to put down the rebellion. There is much more, of people, time and events, all woven in a tapestry of historical fact that is interlaced with fictitious interludes to balance the readability of the novel.

Written history is not the truth; it is someone's perception of a time gone by. The sources for this narration were many. Archives, museums and a host of books provided the information. The best was from an unknown source. Many stories were extracted by travelling through hundreds of remote village trails in Sri Lanka in search of old temples and old men who remembered what they heard.

That in all its simplicity is "The Last Kingdom of Sinhalay", a historical novel written purely from the heart in an unbiased attempt to voice what may have been the truth.

Captain Elmo Jayawardena
Singapore

"The Gratiaen Prize is to celebrate and test and trust ourselves"

- Michael Ondaatje

Sam's Story was a recipient of the Gratiaen Prize for the best literary work in English for 2001, in Sri Lanka. This award is given by the Gratiaen Trust, set up on the initiative of Michael Ondaatjee from the Booker Prize award for his book 'The English Patient' which was later made into a successful film.

The proceeds from the sale of 'Sam's Story' is used for the work of the Association For Lighting A Candle (AFLAC), a charity established by Elmo and his wife Dil to assist the poor in Sri Lanka. Up to June 2002 AFLAC have established and equipped 14 libraries in rural Sri Lanka and award over 200 scholarships to poor children to continue their education. AFLAC also maintains a Ward at the Cancer Hospital in Maharagama for poor patients.

Why Sam's Story was chosen

Sam, the narrator, comes to the city to work as a domestic servant. Through this young boy's encounters, observations and uniquely innocent perceptions, we see the gradual unravelling of the web of fate that seems to pre-determine the life of all – the master, his servants, the dogs, Sam and his friends and the Sinhalese, the Tamils and the society at large. Sam is a young rural boy, who is not formally educated, but extremely sensitive to strange things that happen in the world around him. This strangeness of things around Sam is largely conditioned by Sri Lanka's North – East War and its consequences as felt in Sam's village in the rural Kalutara district as well as in Colombo where he is employed. As a boy without much social exposure, Sam has a certain original quality of unsophistication, which borders on naivety. The accidental death of Sam's master in a suicide bomb attack in Colombo brings to an end the world of small rivalries between Sam and his co-workers in a revelation that perplexes Sam. He goes back to his village and contemplates on the inexplicable predicament that befell on all former dwellers of the river house.

Sam says, "My master had nothing to do with this stupid war and nothing against anybody on either side. He had no comment to make about all this business of dividing the country and who should get what part. He only said, 'It was all meaningless.' He just drank his Russian and watched his fish eating their green balls and went about carrying people in his 'aerobblane'..... We were all defeated by this stupid war that none of us had anything to do with."

In short, Sam's Story is a novel that makes a noteworthy contribution to English fiction in Sri Lanka by pointing towards a mode of literary practice that is socially and politically meaningful as well as vibrant in its capacity for critical reflection.

-Dr. Jayadeva Uyangoda, Chairman of the selection panel, speaking on behalf of the judges announcing their decision at the Gratiaen Prize award ceremony on June 1, 2002

Critical acclaim for Sam's Story

"It is a story told simply and with genuine concern".

Romesh Gunasekara, Author (Monkfish Moon, Sandglass and Heaven's Edge)

"It has the hallmarks of a classic - simple and powerful, much in the vein of Hemingway's *Old Man & the Sea* ".

Sam Bunny, Editor/Contract Publisher

"A vastly sensitive and gripping experience of the "other" within and without the context of the "one". The natural responses of native intelligence to forces that claw out for primacy puts the traumas of a sunburnt island into the sensibilities of the uneducated narrator. The effect is startling and, above all, near surrealistic; wholly absorbing".

Carl Muller, First winner of Gratiaen Award

"Sam's Story is Jayawardena's debut. Narrated by the boy Sam who comes from a remote village to work in Colombo, Sam's Story is about the poor man's concept of the ethnic conflict".

Sunday Times